PURSUIT OF A BETTER LIFE

PURSUIT OF A BETTER LIFE

Rx for MHM from Dr. Brad

Martha H. Mulinix

authorHOUSE®

AuthorHouse™ LLC
1663 Liberty Drive
Bloomington, IN 47403
www.authorhouse.com
Phone: 1-800-839-8640

Narrator: MHM
Scribe: Eugenia Sherman
Scribe: Misty Nuckols
April 2012-January 2013

Published by AuthorHouse 11/26/2013

ISBN: 978-1-4918-3925-6 (sc)
ISBN: 978-1-4918-3923-2 (hc)
ISBN: 978-1-4918-3924-9 (e)

Library of Congress Control Number: 2013921783

This book is printed on acid-free paper.

TABLE OF CONTENTS

FOREWORD

The following is a one page document that My mother wrote which helps to explain her mental state in her last days as she wrote this book. I quit work in 2009 and spent the last years of my father's and mother's life trying to help them live in the environs and lifestyle that made them comfortable.

Victor f. Mulinix

My life is **Gone.**

. . . and I did not achieve the aspirations of my youth:

To **READ EVERYTHING**:

Macular degeneration stopped me

To **Travel—Everywhere**

Arthritis, age, compression fractures stopped me

BUT . . . LIFE HAS BEEN GOOD

I thank God for:

. . . growing up in a hard-working Christian home and having the opportunity for an education that emphases the simple things of life

. . . marring my teen years sweetheart who after 60^{+} years still tells me each day that he loves me

. . . having a healthy family who grew up with an abiding "work ethic" that even in our grandsons shows an appreciation for family values

NOW—leaving MANY unfinished projects

with the knowledge that family, friends and former students can—and will carry on M M Aug 2010

Chapter One

PURSUIT OF A BETTER LIFE

Stephen Washington, (S. W.), and Viley Ann Tate Puryear were my grandparents. The second of their daughters, Lula, was my mother. She was married to John F. Hefner, youngest son of T. D. Hefner, who lived on the opposite end of the Valley, which is in "the Pocket" area of nothern Floyd county.

S. W. and Viley had ten girls. The flu epidemic took an aunt. Her daughter came to live with S. W. and Viley making eleven girls. There were three boys but one, Leo, died in childhood.

Education was very important to S. W. He never had "much schoolin'" as he said, so it was always very important to him that his children get as much education as he could provide.

In the community of Zone, it was customary for the young men to go away for school. One of the young men attended Martha Berry School for Boys for a short while. My daddy, John Hefner, went across the mountain to Sugar Valley and attended a facility directed by a Professor Pittman. One of the girls attended boarding school, but for the most part, there was no schooling available for girls beyond seventh grade.

A normal class consisted of all ages and was taught by one or two teachers in a one-room schoolhouse or in the local church. Some of the girls were able to take a state exam and became certified to teach, like Velma and possibly Ione. Three or four of S. W.'s girls, who had only finished seventh grade, married local boys. This bothered S. W.; he wanted more for his girls.

Move to LaFayette

Ever on the lookout for schooling opportunities for girls, S. W. heard that the schools in La Fayette offered classes for grades one thru high school at no cost to residents of LaFayette. He was excited and began making plans and preparations to move at least a part of his family to LaFayette. John and Lula could handle the store and the Zone Post Office in his absence. They could also care for the animals and make contact with the tenant farmers on his property.

The result was a purchase of a house and lot and a move to the section of LaFayette called Sunnyside. Along with the family, S. W. took one cow, one mule, a wagon, tools for gardening, and a flock of chickens. It was in the early 1900's that S. W. started a routine of taking all of his school age children, and as many of his grandchildren as would go, to LaFayette. The car, loaded with children would leave Zone on Sunday afternoon in order to be in school on Monday. On Friday they would leave LaFayette and go back to the farm in Zone to do the chores required to keep the farm going.

In LaFayette, he established a milk route for the local area. His deliveries included milk, butter, eggs and a variety of fruits and vegetables brought from the farm. Soon he acquired a larger lot on N. Main Street with room for a larger garden and his chickens and cow.

Velma, John and Lula's first child, was one of the grandchildren to take advantage of this education arrangement. She started first grade in 1918. She loved school, but missed her mom and dad and their long talks about everything. It was especially hard in 1922 when her mom was expecting a baby.

S. W.'s Dream Unfolding

Summertime meant full time working at the farm from sun up to sun down. One summer day a representative from Berry School visiting in the area stopped by the farm. The family knew of the work oriented school for boys near Rome, but this representative was looking to enroll girls only. She urged S. W. to send his girls to Berry and suggested that one girl could go with her when she left the next day.

After much discussion, three girls were considered to be eligible. Each held a Certificate for grade 1-7. The three were small, which meant clothes could be modified to fit so that they had the necessary dresses. The final choice was based mainly on the fact that the smallest girl had the only pair of wearable shoes. The one chosen was Ione.

The oil lamps burned late into the night scouring around for and modifying clothes. She would need at least a week's worth. Although it was taxing on all concerned, S.W. believed if educational opportunities could furnish a rite of passage to a more satisfactory life, it was worthwhile.

Grandma was up early that morning fixing a big breakfast and a basket of food to go in the buggy. Before the sun came up over the mountain, the carefully loaded buggy and its occupants were on their way.

The road to Rome was very familiar to the Berry representative. She had spent many days visiting farms and homesteads along the way. As a result the enrollment for Martha Berry School for Girls grew steadily. Travel was slow and the conversation was light. Uncertainty about what was ahead and the first time away from home and family, left no desire to chit chat. They arrived at the school just as the sun began to set. A group of students stood around a bonfire welcoming weary new arrivals and helping locate their living quarters.

Sharing the Dream

At the end of the school session, Ione came back to work on the farm and preparations were made for another girl to take her place for the next session. Since the children were needed to work on the farm, this seemed to S.W. to be a fine plan. They did this for a number of years. It was fine for the farm, but it didn't work so well for a student trying to meet the requirements for graduation. As far as I know, none of the girls following this swap-out procedure ever graduated. However, they learned many things that influenced them for the rest of their lives. Almost all of them sent their own children to Berry in later years. Ione's daughter, Mary Elizabeth, told me just recently, that her mother had worked in the La Fayette School for several years.

Hints of Change

Weekends at home with the family were always special. However, this weekend Velma sensed something different. First, the schedule was more flexible—no more regular classes for two months.

Soon, when the car came into Zone and turned into their driveway, the doctor was right in front of them. He appeared to be going to the barn to put up his horse as though he would be spending the night.

Also, cousin Tom was waiting at the store. He asked Velma if she would like to spend the night with Nancy and him. She usually had to beg to go to Tom and Nancy's. Today, she was told she could go without even asking and told they would gather some roast 'n' ears.

Velma's mother, Lula, was not in the store. Her younger sister, Bertha, was minding the store and the Zone Post Office. She said Lula Velma's mother, was resting. Could it be that Lula's time had come? The baby that they had talked about for months must be due.

Daddy John came through the store, gave Velma a quick kiss on the top of her head and announced to no one in particular, "I'm going for Mother Hefner." That was the final hint. Mother Hefner always helped the doctor when a local baby was born. Yes! It had to be. She quickly counted on her fingers—exactly nine months! She remembered the conversations she had with daddy and mother, they had figured that some time in June would probably be the due date.

The Announcement

Next morning, June 23, 1922, when Tom and Velma had gathered a load of corn, they stopped at the barn to shuck and silk it. As they walked down the road to take the corn to the cook, they saw Daddy John literally prancing along the smooth, hard, chert road that was a part of his county assessment to keep up. He took seriously his responsibility to keep this section of the road in good shape.

His prancing became dancing; his steps turned into buck dancing like his daddy had done. When he saw Tom and Velma, he cupped both hands over his mouth and shouted, "It's a girl!" They named me Martha Frances, but Velma called me "My Dollie" and often lined me up with the rest of her dolls.

I thrived and stayed in my "Goods Box" (a wooden crate emptied of the goods), playing and reacting to anyone who came into the store during the long, hot, dry, summer.

Through the years, S.W.'s dream unfolds—

Velma Graduated Berry College in 1939

Martha Frances graduated Berry High School in 1940 and Berry College in 1944.

Regretfully this is written about 50 years too late for the writer to have clear and precise memories of the story.

CHAPTER TWO

HARD TIMES

The Zone community was not faring so well. Field crops and pastures dried up; most crops were total failures. Many springs had gone dry. Wildlife, as well as farm animals, were suffering. When it came time for farmers to settle accounts, they had nothing to settle with.

Another year or two of drought, no crops, and no settling of accounts caused S. W. to turn all responsibility for settling the store's debt over to John. Because he felt he was illiterate, S. W. would not sign any legal documents. John had to go to the bank and borrow funds to re-stock the store and carry on farming operations. John also secured some nearby land and worked to build a new house on it. People began leaving the valley—many never to return.

Desperate Times—Desperate Measures

John needed more income than the store was providing. He acquired a truck and used his driving ability to work with sawmills and timber cutters whenever he could, to try and "make ends meet". He hauled logs for sawmills and lumber companies, while Lula carried on at the store the best she could. Within a year, John disposed of almost everything but still lacked the means to support the operations in Zone

Because John was driving far and late into the night, and Velma was in LaFayette during the week for school, Mother Hefner came to help Mother with me. They never knew how late John would be getting home. Mother Hefner always worried about him. She paced the floor thinking out loud, "He may have had a flat tire. He may be stuck in the mud or he may have run off the road or encountered some other road hazard." Mother often said she and I would have been better off without Mother Hefner's floor walking. It kept me awake and that meant that Mother was awake also.

Mother Hefner also worried about me because I had begun to make a few one-syllable words. She reminded Mother of the wives tale, "Girls that talk before they walk," and tied it in with "Whistling girls and crowing hens will likely come to no good end."

A New Life on the Railroad

Perry Puryear, one of Mother's brothers, could not see an end to the drought conditions and became one of those looking for "greener pastures" elsewhere. He moved his family to Mogul, just outside of Macon, Georgia, where there was a rail yard with several tracks which converged and intersected. There were at least two track foremen in this area. Perry began working on the Central of Georgia Railroad in Mogul.

Two years later, when Perry returned to visit family in the Valley, he saw how difficult things were for John. He convinced John that he would be able to find a job with the railroad. So, in the early 1920's, John gave up the store in Zone. When Perry returned to Mogul, John went with him and began working with Central of Georgia Railroad, too. He moved his family to Mogul, next door to Perry and began working as a "rail hand" on a section in training under Perry. Sometime later, Perry went to Detroit to work in an ammunition plant. John stayed with the railroad until he retired.

Brighter Days

John learned the ropes quickly and was soon made Foreman of an Extra Gang. He had his own crew of up to thirty-five men and three Apprentice Foremen. They went to trouble spots and helped get things "back on track", so to speak. One time a massive wash out destroyed both lines of a long double track line in Wadley. Daddy John's Gang was assigned to get the tracks open as soon as possible. John and his Gang worked night and day to repair the tracks. It was John's responsibility to issue the "Go Ahead" on Section 7 track. He often walked the track through standing water ahead of a slow moving engine to determine if it was safe. Sometimes he rode on the "cow catcher". Nothing was allowed to move until it had his clearance.

The long hours of hard work took its toll on John's back. He left his Apprentice Foremen in charge and began spending the nights at a nearby boarding house.

He had a string of camp cars—one for himself as Foreman; one for cooking, dining, and recreation; and one or more for sleeping quarters for his crew. However, the bunk provided for him only seemed to aggravate his back. Although sleeping on the bed at the boarding house was easier on his back, he did not like leaving his crew. He bought a single bed and put it in the camp car; he said being back with his crew made him feel better.

While still in Mogul, John was reassigned as Section Foreman over his own section of tracks. Velma had not moved with the family to Mogul, but stayed to finish the school year in LaFayette. When school let out for the summer, she joined the family in Mogul.

Home in Time to Move

Almost immediately, because of the unsettled times with the railroad, Daddy John was sent on a different assignment to Willard, Georgia, a small community just outside Eatonton, in Putnam County. During an assignment as Extra Gang Foreman, our family lived in Eatonton and he was only home on weekends. There was no public transportation from Willard to Eatonton where Velma would go to school. They learned that a neighbor was a teacher at Eatonton High. As the two families became acquainted, they worked out an arrangement with her to get Velma to school. The teacher, Elizabeth Rainey, came each day and took Velma to school.

As Foreman of an Extra Gang, Daddy John again had his foreman's car, the cook and dining car, and the cars for the crew, but there was no provision made for his family. We had to stay where we were in Eatonton, until he found a house we were able to share with an elderly lady named Augusta Ross. She had a big lot and a barn with plenty of room for mother's cow.

To our regret, Mrs. Augusta received notice from the city zoning board that the cow on her property had to be removed. She tried very hard to get the order rescinded, but to no avail. So Daddy John moved us to another house which was about twice as far from the school as the first house.

A Trip Home

When my mother was pregnant with her third child, over and over I heard the expression, "She's expecting." It made me wonder, "Expecting what?" In the spring before the baby was born, my mother spent a lot of time with me. She explained that there were a lot of old wives tales which attempted to ascertain the sex of the baby. These were not true—unlike the present time when doctors can determine the sex of the expected child. Mother explained, "We just have to wait until the baby is born to see if you have a little sister or brother."

Mother began to teach me this poem:

"Jesus loves the little children,
All the children of the world.
Red and yellow, black and white,
They are precious in His sight.
Jesus loves the little children of the world.

May 18, 1927, my sister Jo was born. It was right at the end of the school year and Mama decided to visit Grandmother Puryear in Zone as soon after school let out as she was able. Nancy, the wife of one of Daddy John's workmen, helped her get ready to go and traveled with us to help care for us. However, when we boarded the train, Nancy was assigned to the black coach and Mother, Jo and I were assigned to the white day coach. Jo became fretful with Mama. The conductor said Nancy could not come to the white coach, "but the children may go to her coach." So Jo and I rode with Nancy in the black coach.

Grandpa Puryear picked us up at the station. On the way home he picked up some ice to make ice cream. As beds were being assigned, S. W. made a casual, but careless remark, that Nancy was the first black person to ever spend the night in the Valley. It upset Nancy and she went to the room which had been assigned to her and lay down on the bed. Soft sobs were heard coming from Nancy's room. Roland, my cousin, took his bowl of ice cream to share with Nancy. Shortly her sobs changed to a gentle tune of "Jesus Loves the Little Children All the children of the world. Red & Yellow, Black and White, they are precious in his Sight, Jesus loves the little children of the world." When they began to look for me, they found me in

Nancy's room, trying to console her. Nancy, Roland, and I rejoined the others still singing "Jesus loves the little Children".

For the remainder of the week, Grandpa tried to make amends and before we left at the end of the week, Nancy and Grandpa were big buddies. Nancy enjoyed the country, the animals, and the vegetable and flower gardens. It was so peaceful and relaxing.

School at Last

The following year, 1928, I started to school; Velma was still in high school, and it was the year Grandmother Hefner died. Velma had gotten her driver's license in September and had begun to drive us to school. When Mother and Daddy John were preparing to go to Grandmother's funeral, they made arrangements with Mrs. Augusta for Velma and me to stay with her so we would not have to miss school. Jo went with Mother and Daddy.

Mrs. Rainey seemed to enjoy my company and appreciated my eagerness to learn. She had grandchildren who would come to her house and play "Snake in the Gulley" with me. When Velma had after-school activities, she would take me to the Library to wait until Mrs. Rainey's teaching duties were complete. Mrs. Rainey would come by the Library to pick me up and take me home. It was on these trips home that Mrs. Rainey would tell me "Uncle Remus" stories and taught me to understand the distinctive language with which Joel Chandler Harris presented the stories of B'rer Rabbit and the other creatures.

Rolling, Rolling, Rolling

It seemed every time I made new friends, Daddy John was given a new assignment and we had to move. This time we moved to Tennille, Georgia. In Tennille, the different size houses provided by the railroad were lined up in a row. First, the Section Foreman's house, which had six to eight rooms and was a one-family residence. Next, the Apprentice Foreman's house was a modified version of the duplex housing provided for crewmen. It had a kitchen, three other rooms, and a large closet. This was our house when Daddy John's father, Grandpa Hefner, came to live with us.

In the spring of 1929, before the end of the school year, Daddy John was moved to McIntyre. The family had to stay in a boarding house until the retiring Foreman moved out of the Foreman's house. Velma stayed in Eatonton to finish out the school year and graduate. She joined the First Baptist Church of Eatonton, the family went to her baptism. This was the first inside baptistery I had ever seen. All other baptisms, including my own, were outside in a lake, creek, or pond.

Rolled Again

The railroad's practice of promotions based on seniority, or "rolling", again moved Daddy John to a new assignment as Apprentice Foreman. The house provided by the railroad was really too small for our family since Grandpa Hefner had joined our family. Mrs. Barton, the retiring Foreman's wife, had started building a house in Burke County. It was the house she hoped to live in when her husband retired. For some reason, work on the house had stopped. The materials were there, but no workers. She approached Daddy John about finishing the work on the house in exchange for a place to live on the farm. He accepted and moved the family to Route #1, Munnerlyn, on Mrs. Barton's property.

Purchase of a Home Place

Mrs. Barton's son, who lived in Augusta, had learned of the house being built by his mother and voiced his concern that the house she had started was not a good place for them to retire. It was too isolated, too far away, and at this time in their lives, they needed to be closer to him. He must have persuaded them, because, somehow Daddy John and Velma bought the house on Barton Hill.

Using the materials already there, Daddy John put in a tongue and groove ceiling in two rooms and left two rooms with unfinished boards. Instead of having a hallway running the length of the house, he left out a partition and made a big bedroom for Lula and himself with the front door opening into it. Some time later, 1944 or '45, Mother and I ordered some wall paper insulation from Sears Roebuck and "nailed" it to the walls.

Looking for Grandpa

Grandpa Hefner had come to the new house at Barton Hill as he was living with us and Daddy John was away with his Extra Gang. One morning, Mother was cooking breakfast; I was still in bed, but Grandpa Hefner had gotten up early, as usual, without disturbing anyone or being seen. He always got up and took his potty to the outhouse to empty it. He was not familiar with the area and must have gotten lost or just decided to explore and couldn't find his way back. When we called him to breakfast, we found out he was not there. We started searching for him. We walked down the dusty road following his footprints in the dust and found his potty by a fence gate. At least we were on the right trail.

Plantation Plain House

The center of the Barton Place was on a hill. One could take about 5 or 6 field roads spiraling out like the spokes of a wagon wheel and get to a neighbor in about a mile or less. One road took you to a "Plantation Plain" house which, community gossip says the present occupants still held a grant from the King of England. The house was a well-built six room house with a "detached kitchen" plus the "preacher's room" or guest room, jn which a bed was either made up or had fresh linens ready to be made up. The only door opened onto the front porch. There was also a porch all across the back of the house. In one end of the kitchen there was a table with chairs at the ends and benches on both sides. At the other end of the kitchen was the stove, ice box, and the sink. Pots and pans hung all around. This was the home of Jim and Lily Brenson. His mother lived with them; I remember the first time I saw her, thinking she was ancient, because of her terribly wrinkled skin. When she died, my daddy and a few other men made her coffin. Velma found some black silk material and stuffing and made a pillow for her head. She also arranged some flowers for her. I remember there was no hearse. The coffin was carried on the back of a logging truck. At the church, Green Forks Baptist Church, they backed as close as they could and the pallbearers carried the coffin to the grave site with all the men's hats stacked on top.

Mandy

A short way from the house stood a one room cabin with the remains of a stick and dirt chimney. There were five or six houses which showed similar remains. The only occupied cabin was near the house of Victor and Lessie Reeves. The occupant was a black woman named Mandy, who wore men's shoes and made the rounds of most of "the big houses" to help on scheduled wash days.

The sun was coming up and things were stirring at the Brenson household; the smell of breakfast cooking was in the air. As we neared the home of Victor and Lessie Reeves, a former teacher in a one-room school house, the dogs began to bark, and Mandy came out to see what was wrong with the dogs. She looked us over, came up to Mother and asked, "You got a wash woman?" Mother said, "Not yet." Mandy asked, "What day you wash?" Mother replied, "Monday." "No, dat's Miz Lessie's day," protested Mandy. "Tuesday?" asked Mother. "Dat should be fine," agreed Mandy, "'bout daylight." "How much do you charge?" Mother inquired. "No money. Just vittles," was her reply. The ladies who used Mandy's services knew her schedule. She had some regulars, like mother became, and some who only used her occasionally. Each one would not only feed her when she worked, but packed extra food for her to take with her until her next work day. Mother agreed and thanked Mandy then turned toward the house where Mrs. Reeves had come onto the porch. Mother introduced herself and asked Mrs. Reeves if she had seen an elderly man wandering around. She explained we had just moved to the house on Barton Hill and Grandpa was not familiar with the area or anyone in it. We had followed his trail to their house. Mrs. Reeves said, "Yes, we saw him wandering around out here. He didn't seem to know where he was or where he lived. My husband was going into town and said he would take Grandpa with him and maybe someone in town would know him."

Mother thanked her and said Daddy John would check back by there when he got off work. Mr. Reeves, in the meantime, had taken Grandpa Hefner to all the stores in Munnerlyn and no one knew anything about him. He took Grandpa to Waynesboro. Someone recognized the Confederate Insignia he was wearing on his jacket lapel. The Postmaster knew the Hefner name and recalled Daddy

John saying something about receiving mail for his father. One of Daddy John's workers said Daddy John had said something about his father coming to live with him. Finally, Mr. Reeves decided to take him back home with him and wait for someone to come for him. Grandpa Hefner just settled in and visited until Daddy John came to take him home.

"Fishing"

One day Grandpa was walking along the creek, when he saw some large turtles sunning on the bank. He had never been "fishing" for turtles. So Daddy John hired a teenage boy, Ted Snow, as a guide and companion to take him "fishing" for turtles. They fixed a trap by placing a stick in the ground and putting hooks on it around the top and baited it with chicken livers. They fixed it so the turtle had to crawl up to get the bait, but would not be able to go back down to the water. Later, when they checked the trap, they had caught a huge turtle. It weighed more than they could carry. They tied a rope to it, turned it over on its back and pulled it to the general store to put on the scale. I don't remember how much it weighed but it was the biggest turtle grandpa ever caught. He took it home, cut the head off, trimmed the meat out of the shell and cooked it. He buried the shell in the garden to let it decay for about a year to help clean the inside and outside of the shell. He had intended to dig it up later. However, once again, the railroad intervened.

Birthday Celebration

We never knew Grandpa Hefner's exact birth date or his exact age. However, with her usual planning and preparation, Velma planned a birthday celebration for Grandpa Hefner. We thought his birthday was in June. Velma found a round tray to serve as a cake pan, covered it very carefully with wax paper, and mixed up enough batter to fill the tray. Mother usually kept little birthday candles in a can. Velma put every candle she could find on the cake. When she lit the candles, it's a wonder we didn't burn the house down—but we didn't. Grandpa Hefner was in his best suit. His snow-white hair and moustache were neatly combed and trimmed. His Confederate medals were shining on his coat lapel.

The Unmarked grave

When Grandpa Hefner died, the Lewis Brothers Hardware in Waynesboro made the funeral preparations. You could see coffins and other funeral items on display in an upstairs room of the store. They prepared his body. They had a hearse which they backed up to our front porch. The wheels made a deep track that was visible for a long time after. The body was not brought back to the house, but taken to the Habersham Methodist Church where the funeral was held; he was buried in the church cemetery. The double marker for him and Grandmother Hefner was in Subligna, where she was buried. No permanent marker was placed on his grave. Different ones in the family wanted his body moved to where the marker was, but no one had the means to pay for such a move. In the early 1960's, Mulinix, with Pop Reeves help, located the grave and took some concrete and poured a flat head stone on the grave since it was in the path between two other graves. He then took a piece of stainless steel and etched the name and necessary information on it and placed it on his new grave marker.

The name "Subligna" means "Sub" under, and "Ligna" wood. The community name was Underwood. Was the name picked randomly or was it descriptive of how some of the graves were done? It is interesting to note that some of the graves had a wooden covering (or were under wood). They were buried in the usual way then a wooden frame was placed on top of the grave. Just such a frame was placed on the grave of Velpo Reeves, son of Victor & Lessie Reeves. Velpo had drowned in the same millpond in which I had been baptized. A friend I went to Sunday School with, Doris Butler, and I would wander through the graveyard reading the tombstones. Doris swore, "If you look right here through this crack, you can see Velpo's toes!"

Memories at Barton Hill

Generally, the wells were very shallow and many times the water was murky. The well at Barton Hill was the exception. It was deeper than any around and was always cool. The water was drawn by a windlass and a rope. It was at the edge of the yard about twenty feet from a huge Chinaberry tree. Drinking water was carried to the house in a cedar bucket. It was amazing how many things went on at that big shade tree by the well

WASHING: Tuesday was our family's wash day set up by Mandy. She came early and built the fire under the wash pot. Mother always insisted that everything be turned inside out to wash, rinsed through two waters, squeezed out and hung on the line to dry. Clothes dried and were carried in before dark.

BARBER: On most Saturday mornings the tree became the site for community hair cuts. Daddy John was the "barber". By the time he arrived at the tree, a group, mostly men and boys, but sometimes a mama would come with two or more kids and want Daddy to cut their hair. She would stay and suggest how she wanted it cut.

HOG KILLING: About twice a year Daddy John killed a hog. He met a couple who lived between us and Munnerlyn who were good help at hog killing time. Daddy always asked them to help which they did. When they had finished, Daddy John always pulled this same tease—"Does your family like the back bones?" "Oh yes," they would say. Then Daddy would count off on his fingers, "Today is Friday, Saturday, Sunday, Monday—I think my family will be done with the bones by then. Why don't you drop by Monday." "Aw, Mr. John, you always pull that on me . . ." they would reply.

FELLOWSHIP: Saturday was a fun time of stories and other activities; Daddy John even sang. The crowd would take turns speaking up; there was one particular man who usually spoke out. Every time the man got started, Daddy John would suddenly ask me to go do something he had promised to do for Mother. Try as I might, I could never get back to the tree before I heard ultra laughing, which meant that particular speaker had finished his story. I've often wondered what it was that Daddy John didn't want me to hear.

One of Daddy's favorite tales: There was a man who lived in the community who drove around with a one-horse wagon and traded or sold produce. (The people knew what he was doing, but they just went along.) He cussed all the time. One day, as the story goes, the wagon was empty. He went to a man who had a large patch of corn. He asked, "What cha gonna do with all that corn?" "I guess I'll give some of it away," the farmer replied. "Give it away? We'll take some." The farmer picked him a generous arm load and put it in his wagon. "Thanks," said the man. Next, the man stopped at a lady gathering tomatoes and asked, "You gonna use all them tomatoes?" "Oh, no. You may have some of them if you like," the woman replied. The next stop didn't want any of his vegetables, but he gave him a bushel of beautiful red apples. The man poured them into the bed of his wagon and started off. "You know that steep hill, that really steep hill before the county worked on it?" Daddy asked. "When he came to that hill, the mule was pulling really hard and somehow that wagon gate came open and apples started sliding off the wagon, rolled downhill and spread out everywhere. The man just stood there without saying a word. Two neighborhood boys came running up. The man still did not say a word. Finally, he looked at the boys and asked, "What do you want?" "We just came to hear you cuss," the boys replied. "No need," he said, "I don't know any cuss words to describe that mess. No, and I guess, to tell the truth, cuss words don't ever tell anything, do they?"

Mandy and the Cow

Mother always had a cow and she would milk her while Mandy drew some water for the cow to drink. When Mother finished milking, and the cow finished drinking, Mother handed her to Mandy, who would take her down the road to the pasture to graze. The story goes that the cow knew the route so well, she actually pulled Mandy down the road while Mandy slept. When she got to the gate of the pasture, she would stop and Mandy would open the gate and let her in to graze.

Advances in Education

In her senior year at Eatonton High School, Velma had applied to Georgia Southern College for Women in Milledgeville, Georgia. She received a letter requesting a personal interview. Daddy John drove her to Milledgeville. As fate would have it, there was a train collision back in McIntyre. It was not on John's tracks but because John could not be found, the superintendent fired him on the spot. They found out later that this particular superintendent did not have the authority to fire him and the railroad never had an official record of him being fired. However, on the railroad someone with more seniority could "roll" someone with less seniority and this happened to Daddy John, quite often.

In the summer after Velma graduated from Eatonton, she organized a study group of young people. They would choose a subject, learn what they could and then choose another subject. The group of ten or twelve would take turns hosting and always looked forward to meeting at Velma's house. She prepared snacks and gave them exotic names pertaining to the subject being studied. For instance, an "Exotic Greek Sandwich" was actually yesterday's leftover squash.

Velma could always make something from something else. I remember one time we were going to have a short skit at school. The girls were to wear white crepe dresses. The teacher sent instructions home on how to make a dress out of crepe paper. Velma did not have any crepe paper and no white material. She took one of Mother's white night gowns and made me a white dress. I wore it to school. The other girls wore their regular clothes and put the crepe dresses on over their dresses for the skit. The play went fine.

Afterward, the teacher let us go out to play. I was running and this little boy began to chase me. He caught up with me and grabbed hold of the back of my collar and stopped. I kept going. It tore a piece the width of his hand all the way down my dress. When the teachers looked at it one said, "It's a new dress but it looks like it's been washed, sort of like it has been made out of something else."

I spoke up and said, "My sister is always making something out of something else." The teacher pinned my dress together as best she could. When I got off the school bus, I tried to explain to Mother and Velma how it happened. Velma started in on me and said, "If you had been acting like a lady should act, this would not have happened . . . ." and on and on and on until finally Mother calmly spoke up, "Velma, I think she understands." Not another word was spoken. I don't know what happened to the dress; I don't remember ever seeing it again.

Velma had been accepted to and attended Georgia Southern College for Women but she did not adjust to dormitory and school life very well. She would stay up all night studying; she would not eat when it was time to eat. The school found her conduct disruptive to the other students. By the end of 1929, the school sent her home with the strong suggestion to get her some medical help. The first doctor she went to, a railroad doctor, diagnosed her with one word—"CRAZY". He offered to help Daddy John with the paper work to get her into the asylum. Daddy John said, "No!" and he never saw that doctor again.

Life Changing Decision

Someone referred him to a doctor in the next town of Sandersville. He never gave a diagnosis, but instructed the family on how to help her work through this difficult time. They were to let Velma alone, let her do things the way she wanted, and they were not to argue with her. From then on, Velma ruled. Mother never contradicted her or called her down in any way. She would not let Velma spank me, but anything else Velma said was done.

It was about this time, late 1930 or early 1931, that Velma decided the family should go to the 1933 World's Fair in Chicago. The family had never been on a vacation together. Velma began planning everything and making the arrangements. Usually, Mother would get the railroad maps and studied them for the shortest route and then get the tickets. This time, the railroad planned the route. Velma's planning was put on hold in 1931, when grandpa Hefner died.

Unknown to Velma, Grandmother Puryear was also planning one last gathering of her children at Zone—the Store place—in 1933. No registration was kept of those who attended, but many years later, Florence, Mother, and I took the two group photographs made by the photographer Grandmother had hired and compiled what is accepted as THE LIST. Ella was absent. Her husband, John Smith, had a very bad sawmill accident and died a short time afterward. The reunion took place first and only lasted four days. Velma's plans were not affected. She even got Daddy John to wear a new plaid suit and plaid cap, in place of his felt hat.

One of the cities we went through was Memphis, Tennessee where we came into possession of a brochure of the "Great River Road". I decided then and there that I wanted to go on this trip which was to the source of the Mississippi. In Memphis the water was backed up to the track, but the train was able to get through. It was not crowded on the train so we each had a seat all our own; we just curled up and went to sleep. Two days and one night on the train and we arrived in Chicago. We got our tickets and went to the fairgrounds. The railroad station was the meeting place at the end of the day. Daddy John managed to find a booth or store and bought, meat, drinks, treats and some kind of bread with poppy seeds on it. We had a very nice picnic, but I never cared for anything with poppy seeds again.

A Long Road Back To Reality

Velma remained under a doctor's care for some time, but gradually began to get better. People who knew her thought she was very intelligent and a very resourceful person. Few people ever knew anything was wrong with her. I stayed with Velma wherever she went. At that time, Velma was driving Daddy John's two-seater Roadster. She would go somewhere and forget, or get confused, about how to get back home. It was my job to get her back home and I always did.

When a friend of ours in the community died, Velma and I went to the home to pay our respects to the family. Velma noticed there were no flowers anywhere around the casket. She and I went back home where Velma got some variegated canes and some wild flowers and made an arrangement on the back of the car. She took it apart and put it in the car. We went back to the family's house and rearranged the canes and wild flowers on the casket. When Velma was pleased with it, she went into the kitchen to help prepare the meal. When it was ready to serve, we went home.

Opportunity at the Pocket
Late 1933-34

Velma decided she wanted to visit our grandparents in Zone. The doctor agreed and said it might be good for her to have a change in her routine. While she was visiting, the Superintendent of Floyd County Schools came to the Valley to figure out some way to get "The Pocket" School going. He made Velma aware of a test she could take to become certified to teach if she was interested. She decided to take the test and did real well on it. The Superintendent offered her immediate employment and she signed on to teach at "The Pocket" School in Floyd County—a primitive building used for school as well as religious services. This position lasted about a year as she helped prepare students to enter Berry—some of whom were her cousins.

Dreams of Being a College Student

While teaching at "The Pocket", Velma decided she wanted to go back to college. She filled out an application and sent it to Berry College. She also turned in her resignation at the end of the school year to the Superintendent of Floyd County Schools.

In 1938, Grandpa, S. W. Puryear, died and the property at Zone and other parts of the Valley were sold. It was later developed into the CCC Camp, an organization set up as a response to the depression. Young men, not otherwise eligible for the Draft, were recruited and employed in conservation activities. They built and repaired roads, constructed bridges and public buildings, and set out trees.

Some members of the family prevailed on Aunt Ella Smith to leave her home and take care of Grandmother. Aunt Ella's husband, John Smith, had just recently died as the result of an accident at the saw mill. Ella was pregnant at the time. Ella agreed and the two of them moved across the mountain to Sugar Valley. This arrangement seemed satisfactory for both of them and none of the Puryear Estate was settled until after Grandmother's death in 1945. At grandmother's death, Ella was given what had been promised before any of the estate was settled. Ella and her small child moved back to Rome where her other children lived.

After Velma graduated from Berry College in 1939, she went to Pennsylvania, to the hospital in Philadelphia, probably on a recommendation from Miss Beverly. For what ever reason, she did not stay more than six or seven months and then went to Savannah to work at the Bethesda Orphanage as a dietitian—a position she had applied for before graduating. She stayed there for about two years.

She was good at organizing and getting things done. That may be why the W.P.A. employed her to set up and maintain a sewing room where local women were given employment to work up fabric supplied by the W.P.A. They made shirts and dresses for the school children of employees and community people who were so far in debt they were in danger of losing their homes. Sewing machines, cutting tables, and other needed items were moved into an empty store building where the ladies worked. It didn't feel as much like a hand out as a helping hand. It was only a short term project, and ended in about four to six weeks.

Chapter Three

AN EXPERIENCE IN FREEDOM

While Velma was still at Grandmother Puryear's, I was allowed to go visit Uncle Bruce and Aunt Florence in Boone County, KY. There were two other girls about my age there, Ellen Holiday and Mary Yates. We were like "the Three Musketeers". We spent a lot of time together. Ellen's brothers were delighted when we found plenty to do on our own and didn't bother them.

Uncle Bruce sang in a men's quartet and was often asked to sing at funerals. On one occasion we three girls attended a funeral with him. During the service a little boy got unruly and his mama carried him out. We went out as well, and managed to get the little boy settled and quiet. His mama left him with us and went back inside. It seems the little boy was a part of the nursery service offered by the GAs—the Girls Auxillary—a mission organization of the Baptist Church for young girls. Their leader was Mary Christine Stephens. The GAs kept children during church services and this little boy was familiar with Ellen and Mary.

The most memorable event that happened that summer was when Ellen, Mary and I were leaving Uncle Bruce's house to go to Mary's house. We decided to take a short cut through what we thought was an empty pasture. When we got about half way there, Ellen spotted Longhorn, the community bull, standing under a shade tree in the corner of the pasture. Ellen said, "Run! Let's get out of here!"

Mary grabbed our hands and whispered, "No! We must not move! Just sit down and be still." We tried to think of what we should do next.

It was about noon and time for lunch. The mothers began to wonder where the girls were. Mary's mother called Aunt Florence to see if we were with her. The answer was "No." The question then was, "Where are the girls?"

By now, Uncle Bruce had come in for lunch and so had Mary's daddy. The telephones at all the houses were buzzing on the party line so that the whole community was asking, "Where could they be?"

Meanwhile, we just sat in a circle and prayed for guidance. Our quiet voices were a contrast to the screaming police sirens. First, one and then several chimed in. One voice stood out as Mr. Yates called out, "I see the girls and I see Longhorn standing quietly under that big Walnut tree in the corner near the river.

Soon there was a helicopter hovering overhead. The pilot called out over the bullhorn, "Just sit still until I land." He brought the helicopter down between us and the bull. The second man ran over to us and walked us back to the helicopter. We got in and the helicopter began to rise. When we reached the Yates place, we got out. The pilot went back to pick up his partner. When he returned, he asked, "All ok?" We replied, "All ok." He turned to his partner and said, "Let's head on back to the station."

Time had come for the "Three Musketeers" to go their separate ways. We gave Mary Christine a quick hug of thanks. One girl verbalized their thoughts: "We've made a lot of good memories during our time here." Each girl agreed.

Uncle Bruce was dreading the traffic on the way to the train station in Cincinnati. One of his neighbors told him he didn't have to go to Cincinnati. He could go to the train stop in Ludlow. When we got to the loading ramp in Ludlow, there were two trains sitting there with engines running. The gates were not open yet. The conductor said they would open in about two minutes. One of the trains was a Dixie Flyer—advertised as faster, more comfortable with fewer stops. The other was the regular train that stopped at all the train stops where passengers were waiting.

When the gates opened, the conductor picked up my bag, I picked up my box lunch Aunt Florence had made for me, and he said, "Here we go, Little Lady."

I realized we were heading to the wrong train. I showed him my pass and tried to tell him I did not need to be on the Dixie Flyer he was trying to put me on. It did not make a stop in Macon. He looked at my pass and still put me on the Dixie Flyer.

When the train conductor checked my pass and I pointed out that the Dixie Flyer did not make a stop in Macon, he said, "You are right, Little Lady, but don't you worry. I'll get you on the right train."

As we arrived in Macon, the conductor got my bag, took my hand and led me to the car exit. The train had made an "emergency stop". Arrangements had been made for a cabby to pick me up and take me to the other train stop. The cabby got my bag and box and took me across town and put me on the regular train. He waited with me until the train was about to leave. He waved and I was on my way again.

Daddy John, Mother and Jo were waiting at the stop in Millen. The conductor helped me get my bag and box and get off the train. He began telling Daddy John about my adventure and evidently he thought it was funny. He laughed and laughed. Velma was just arriving on the train from the Valley. I was glad to be home—for about ten minutes—the length of time it took for Jo and Velma to begin bickering with each other. Daddy John said, "Alright now, it's been lonesome around here—a sweet lonesome, but lonesome. Let's see if we can't get along with each other." Mother spoke up and said, "Velma, there's a letter from Berry. Maybe you've been accepted."

Velma had been accepted and in the fall of 1935 she entered Berry College. Her first work assignment was as the assistant to the school nurse, Miss Beverly. Velma took temperatures, blood pressure, and dispensed aspirin. It seemed she had a natural talent for nursing. Eventually, the school nurse designed a white uniform for her to wear.

My Schooling

I went to school in Waynesboro, but did not start at the beginning of the year. Because of so many moves and school transfers, my records were incomplete. I had no report card, no school record, and no adult to escort me and explain it all. I was put back a grade. A year or so later, I was moved up a grade. Evidently, still not sure I was in the "correct" grade they decided to use the new standardized test.

On the day the test was scheduled, there was roadwork between my home and the school. Daddy John had to make a detour and I was very late getting to school. I was handed the test with no instructions on how to complete it and I missed every question. The teacher thought that because I would have been moved to a new and unfamiliar building, and away from my friends; that I had deliberately failed. She took me aside and told me I would not be moved. I stayed with the same group as long as I attended Waynesboro school. I don't remember deliberately failing that test.

I attended Waynesboro through one year of high school. There was no school bus that far out. Daddy John had to take me to Munnerlyn as he went to work. I would catch the school bus to Waynesboro High School from there. This arrangement only lasted until school was out. I actually got to ride the school bus, such as it was. A bus built on a truck body with curtains on the windows, which they closed in the winter to keep the cold air out, and lights in the front only. Sadly, the bus ride stopped when the bus driver shot himself.

During the '36–'37 year of high school in Waynesboro, I filled out an application to Berry High School. Velma was already at Berry in her second year of college. At that time, Daddy John would not sign the application. I could not understand why.

We children went to Sunday School at the Methodist Church. We would walk down to our neighbor's, the Reeves. Mrs. Butler would come by and we would pile in her station wagon which already looked full when she arrived. Along the way she would stop and pick up one or two others. Someone said we rode two or three deep. There were sand beds, two or three between the Reeves' and the church. When it was wet, it made a nice smooth road. But when it was dry—it was shifting sands. The car drove itself, swerving from side to side, like a snake trail. We also attended Green Fork Baptist Church during revivals. Daddy John sang in the choir.

He had a good voice and they loved to see him coming. From his childhood, he had been schooled in shaped notes music. He could read music and timing. When they tried to learn a new song, he was a great help to them.

I joined Green Fork Baptist Church and was baptized in a nearby millpond. Shortly after that, Daddy John signed my application to

Berry and I put it in the mail. It was his belief that until a child reached "the age of accountability", which meant showing a maturity in your relationship and actions toward others, or joining the church and maturing spiritually, the child was his responsibility. When I joined the church, in his eyes, I had become responsible for myself.

A Foot in the Door

I received my letter of acceptance to Berry High School for the '37-'38 school term with the date for me to arrive. Daddy John told me when I picked one bale of cotton and sold it, he would give me the money from it for my school money. I wrote Berry back that I could not possibly come until I had baled and sold at least one bale of cotton. Their reply to me was, "Come as soon as you can and let us know when you will arrive."

Mother had a brother, Pink Puryear, who lived near Rome. She called him and asked him to pick me up at the station and take me to the school. The whole time I was at Berry, if Mother called, he was "Johnny-on-the-spot" to meet my needs. I often asked my mother what she was holding over his head to make him so available.

When I first arrived at Berry, Pink took me to the Dean's office and left me. After talking to me for a few minutes, she told her Office Assistant, "Take this child to Velma Puryear. I stayed with Velma that night in the upper class dorm and she helped me get settled in with my four or five other roommates the next morning. When I entered the room, all I could see was a row of beds against the wall. We shared two closets and two chests of drawers. We had two drawers each and one-third of the closets each.

First semester at Berry High School I was working. When I tried to set my course of study for the second semester, the classes I wanted were not available. I had to take second semester Algebra without the advantage of the first semester Algebra base. I was told by my counselor that I was very lucky. My roommate, Ruby Thompson, was very good in Algebra. As it turned out, she was not as helpful as I had been led to believe.

Working summers paid for the next year and I took advantage of every opportunity. My work schedule was never a regular eight-to-four schedule. It was fragmented between studies, classes, and extra-curricular activities.

I had dated a young upper classman a couple of times, and he had become very possessive. I was not interested in continuing the relationship. At an afternoon reception for welcoming new students, I saw this young man heading straight for me. Standing beside me was my cousin Roland's roommate, Rufus Eugene Mulinix. I asked him if he had a date for the afternoon. He said, "No". I took his arm, whirled him around and said, "Well, you do now," and we headed to Barnwell Chapel. Mulinix never let me forget that I had asked him for our first date.

Chapter Four

TALES RETOLD

Through the years, as time has passed, it is sometimes difficult to tell the difference between tales you lived and those you have been told. For this section of this document, it will be following, as far as possible, the sequence of the houses in which the family lived through unstable times for the railroad.

Mogul I
First move next door to Perry Puryear

I often ran to the car storage shed to get Daddy John's lunch box. I never knew what surprise he might have for me—apples, oranges, even baby rabbits. On this particular day, as the workmen unloaded the motor car, one of the men became aware of a loose engine, (which was an Engine and a coal car), coming into the yard for service. This was Mogul's function—maintenance on the engines and refilling the coal car and the water. I was running straight for my daddy and the surprise he was bringing me, and also right into the path of the loose engine. Screaming whistles, bells, and screeching wheels never got my attention nor changed my course. One of the workmen saw that the engine was not going to be able to stop in time. He rushed over and grabbed me and barely got to the track next to where I had been standing. Holding me in his arms as the engine raced by, I didn't seem to understand the danger I had been in. When he put me down, I headed straight for Daddy John and his lunch box.

Do I remember this? I think about it now, and I can feel the heat of the coal burning engine. I wish I could remember the name of the man who saved my life.

Doll in the Closet

In the Apprentice Foreman's house, we had a large closet. Everything got piled in it. My doll got piled in the closet and I started looking for it. It was so dark in the closet. I got some pages of the Sears Roebuck Catalog, rolled them up, took them to the fireplace and lit them. Then I ran back to the closet to find my doll. The pages of the catalog burned up quickly. So I got some papers and lit them. About that time, someone came in. The only thing that was burned was the fur collar on Velma's coat. I was lucky and only got a strong lecture.

Breaking the Plate

It wasn't uncommon for me to be at Perry's house at mealtime and join the family to eat. One day the family gathered at the table and Uncle Perry pulled the high chair up to the table for me. As food was passed around, Uncle Perry put a big spoonful of something on my plate. I looked at it, picked up the ironstone plate with both hands and threw it on the floor. The boys snickered and Uncle Perry put me down roughly on the floor and popped my bottom. I quickly ran home. It didn't take long for Mother to find out what had happened. She searched through her plates until she found a plate as close to the one I had broken as she could. She made me take it over and apologize to Aunt Fronnie. Years later, Aunt Fronnie gave me a white ironstone plate cracked almost in half. This was the same plate that I had taken over to replace the one I had broken and it rests today in my kitchen.

Mogul II

Moved into larger house—no longer beside Perry. With a new assignment and a Section of his own, Daddy John moved us to the house provided for a Section Foreman. This meant making more new friends. There was a family with several children—one was my age and two were older than I. These new playmates introduced some new activities—one of which was placing a penny or other small object on the track and watch a train run over it. Not only was the penny ruined, but the practice was illegal. These children had made friends with a couple who ran the general store just outside the railroad right-of-way. The older children watched for and gathered freshly laid brown eggs from mother's hen nests. They took them to the store and swapped them for bottled drinks—Orange Crush—their favorite.

The little girl nearest my age was not very well "potty trained". When she had "to go" she "went" in her panties. Then she would take them off and leave them where she took them off and go right on playing.

Mother tried to keep me occupied so I would not have so much time to spend with the neighbors. She let me help with some of the household chores—like making the bed, sweeping the floor, and washing the dishes.

Mother usually did the cooking for the family and much of the housework. As the time neared for the new baby, she needed some help. The wife of one of Daddy John's crew was called in to help. She came each day and was a very good cook. She learned quickly how the family wanted things and even seemed to take delight in having me under foot. One day I was calling off letters on a bucket of something on a shelf in the kitchen. The first letter was big and so elaborate that I was uncertain what it was. After a while I gave up and asked the cook what the letter was. "Law Child," was Cookie's reply, "I don't know. You'll have to ask yo' Pa." I was surprised and suddenly realized that some adults could not read.

Duck Without a Head

Some of the women of the railroad community had organized Sunday School classes for the children. It was big on birthday celebrations. On my fourth birthday I was allowed to sit in a chair specially decorated for me. The teacher gave me a gift. When I opened it, I found a plastic toy duck which no longer had a head. The teacher's son had become curious about what was in the bag. He had taken the scissors and cut the bag open. In doing so, he had cut the head off the duck. I began to cry. The teacher made her son apologize, but it didn't stop my tears.

Rash Reaction

Jo, my younger sister, was born in May. It was very hot and Daddy was taking Mother for a walk just to get her out of the house. I begged to tag along. I saw some beautiful flowering plants ahead of us. I began running through them and smelling the blossoms. It turned out to be "Cow Itch" and I broke out in a rash on my arms, legs, face, and eyes. The home remedy Mother had put on it did not work, so they took me to the doctor. He treated the rash and it began to clear up. But the doctor said, "It may be clearing up now, but this time next year it will reappear. She won't even have to get near it."

Sure enough, for the next three years I broke out with the rash. Never as severe as the first time, but that was when I learned that beautiful plants could be hazardous to my health.

When Jo was born, Velma wanted to name her Elizabeth after Elizabeth Rainey. She had grown very fond of Mrs. Rainey. I could not say Elizabeth. Velma thought of Daddy John's sister, Josephine, and Grandmother Puryear, whose name was Viley Ann. She agreed to the name Viley Josephine, with the stipulation they call her Jo. And so it was. "Jo" is even the name on her tombstone.

Life And Death

We lived within walking distance of the Post Office. I was headed there one morning when I came to an old, but well-kept house. There were some children I enjoyed playing with outside playing. When they saw me they yelled for me to come play. Naturally, I wanted to play, so I joined in their games.

Their father took great pride in his beds of flowers as well as the neat rows of vegetables in his garden. There were some rows of Irish potatoes the children found very interesting. The plants were as high as their heads and had blossoms on the tops. They squealed with delight as they ran up and down the neatly laid out rows of potatoes.

Their father came out of the house, clapped his hands for attention, and yelled out, "Get out of those potatoes! I've just sprayed them. The spray is poison. It will KILL YOU!" The children obediently went to another part of the yard to play. I decided I might need to go on to the Post Office and return home. As I walked in the Post Office the Postmaster told the clerk, "Watch this. She can read." She handed me the mail. I looked through it and handed her back one piece. She looked at the clerk and said, "See there. I told you. She can read." I could not read. But I could recognize the Hefner name. If I did not see the Hefner name, I knew it was not ours and gave it back to the postmaster. I quickly left the Post Office and ran straight home. I walked over to my mother's rocker, climbed up in it and gently rocked, waiting to die. Since I had lost my grandmother Hefner earlier that year, I had become aware that people did not live forever. I understood that when someone died, there were other people who buried them. Still, I had many thoughts and unanswered questions. For instance, "Who would bury the last person to die?"

With the recent birth of a baby sister, I was not sure where babies came from, but I had figured out they did not come in the doctor's black bag.

One-Lane Bridge

There was a covered one-lane bridge between Willard and Eatonton. As you came up the ramp, you had to stay on runners. The bridge sat catty-corner of the river and you had to watch for cars coming around a curve approaching the bridge at the other end. I was supposed to watch and tell Velma when it was clear, but just as Velma drove upon the bridge runners, another car came onto the bridge from the other end and kept on coming. Velma had to back off the bridge and ran off the runners into the bridge railing. She broke the tail light. When we got home, Velma made me tell Daddy John about the tail light. She always made me tell Daddy John when things went wrong.

The Library

Velma would take me to the library to wait for Mrs. Rainey when she had after school activities. She had gotten me a library card so I could check out books. Mrs. Rainey, our neighbor and my ride home on these days, would finish her duties and come by the library for me. There was a special shelf of books for children my age on a lower shelf. One day I decided I didn't want a book from that shelf and I got one from a higher shelf. When I started to check it out, the clerk told me I couldn't because it was too old for me to read. The Librarian happened to be standing nearby and told the clerk, "Let her check it out. When she brings the book back, you can ask any question you want about it and she will be able to answer you. She has someone who reads to her."

The Sugar Bowl

Mother had a large ironstone sugar bowl. Somehow I broke it. I picked up the pieces, took them into the dining room and put them behind the door. When I returned to the kitchen, the cook asked me what I did with the pieces. I told her I had put them behind the door. The cook sort of snickered and asked, "Why did you put them behind the door?" I told her, "To save them for Daddy John. He'll fix it. He can fix anything." When Daddy John came home, I gave him the pieces of the sugar bowl and said, "Fix it." Daddy John looked at me and said, "Sorry, child. I can't fix that." That was when I learned that there were some things even daddy couldn't fix.

TALES REMEMBERED

Unusual Snacks

I was always making friends with neighbors. In one of the houses within view of my house, lived a lady who spent a lot of time in the yard with her flowers. She taught me to eat Nasturtiums and Violets. Another neighbor, the Smiths, grew a plant that looked like an overgrown cucumber. When it matured, if you cut it open, it looked like a sponge. He called it a "Dishrag plant" and the substance inside could indeed be used to wash dishes. Later, I learned it was a Loofah, a tropical gourd.

Grammar Lesson

The one thing I remember learning while in McIntyre was that there are three "to's". There was "t-o", "t-o-o", and "t-w-o". I had used the wrong one in a sentence and the teacher had explained each one to me in detail. I never forgot it.

Seabie's Wedding

When Velma came home from school, she and Seabie Reeves hit it off right away. As usual, Velma began to try to influence Seabie. She began making plans for Seabie's choice of a husband. She encouraged Seabie to consider the son of the Railroad Supervisor, Mr. Waters, for her future husband. Mr. Waters wanted his son to learn the railroad business from the ground up. He put him under Daddy John for training. Velma was able to work on Seabie and on Mr. Waters' son.

When Seabie got married, it was a new experience for me. It was a candlelight service. The church was decorated with brown paper over the big, tall windows and Smilex, an evergreen vine, hanging in vertical rows from the top of the windows to the bottom. The wedding was on her parent's anniversary. Her wedding dress was silver, not the traditional white. When everyone stood up as the bride came in, all I could see was Seabie's little bitty feet as they slipped in and out of her dyed high heel shoes.

"Mind Your Own Business."

The last summer I was at home before I left for Berry High School, I was looking at an old Zone store ledger and found some large accounts that showed no evidence of ever being settled. One in particular caught my attention—the family of a dear friend. I asked Mother if this was the same family of the girl my age that I had enjoyed so much as a child. She just said, "Yes". The next time I was home, I was unable to find the ledger. When I asked mother about it, she just replied, "The ledger is gone and you don't need it."

After some of the dealings the girl told me about and the lifetime contacts between the two families, I decided maybe there really are some tales that should not be re-told. I think my mother would approve if I deliberately omit some things.

Chapter Five

COLLEGE YEARS AND BEYOND

In May 1940, high school was nearing the end. It was time for Class Day where awards for achievements were given and skits were presented. I always enjoyed participating in plays, programs, and chorus. Four of my friends and I put on an impromptu skit spoofing some of the faculty before the awards were handed out. I received two awards. One was for Activities in which I had participated. The second was Scholarship, the Salutatorian. This was an unusual combination. It was rare that one who participated in so many activities also scored high in academics. I was told there was only one point difference between Valedictorian and Salutatorian. When Dean Alston heard about the one point difference, she was so angry, because the boys were not graded on housekeeping. The girls were. I did not have a good housekeeping grade. Mrs. Porter told me, "You are the 'pilingest' girl I've ever seen." (That's true even today.) The low room grades she gave, brought my average down enough that the boy received the Valedictorian award.

Campus Kids went to elementary School at Possum Trot. They knew the quad drills. All freshmen had to have P. E. We (the four girls who graduated with me and I) were put with the Campus Kids. P. E. was the last period in the afternoon. By the time we finished, my legs were so tired and weak I could hardly walk. Later, Moss taught that group some folk dances that others didn't do and never would do.

Pre-graduation celebrations for high school were held in the high school Recitation Hall. Graduation was held at Frost Chapel on Saturday. I had applied for and received a work scholarship. Work students were offered one or two courses which were taught just for them. My first college class began on Monday after graduation. It was an advanced college course in Educational Psychology aimed at seniors and taught by the acting President of the School, Dr.

Green. Imagine being a freshmen and being put in a class primarily for college seniors. I started out behind—no background subjects. I never was sure how much it helped or didn't help, but I got credit for the course and never had to take the course again.

During my senior year of high school, 1939–'40, I was fortunate to have a roommate, dear friend, and future sister-in-law, Louise Russell, who was a local resident. I often stayed in her home because Munnerlyn was too far away to take a weekend trip home. Rome, Georgia and my roommate's home were always a welcome change from school.

When vacation time came, Louise and I rode the train to Millen to visit my family at Munnerlyn. We even made an overnight trip to visit Velma at the Bethesda Orphanage. There was never a dull moment when you were around Velma. She was always trying to learn new things and teach them to me as well. She took us to help catch crabs. To our surprise, those same crabs were served at the dinner table the next day. When we returned to Munnerlyn, we told everybody who would listen about our crab adventure.

At the end of school break, we rode the train back to Rome, Georgia. Louise was going to begin a clerical job and attend a business school. I was returning to Berry College.

Work Begins

I learned that I was to work on the girl's school cleaning crew under the supervision of Mrs. Latham. I was assigned with someone who was experienced so she could teach me what to do. Mrs. Latham gave out assignments and the girls, as they scattered were assigning duties. As she moved on to work with other groups, the girls who already knew what was expected were giving tips to the new girls as to what to do and not do. We were told, "Anytime your supervisor comes around, be sure you are working."

A few days later, I was assigned with the group to clean the bathrooms. Another girl was given a dry mop and told to shine the tiled hall floor. She came into the bathroom and almost immediately, Mrs. Latham came in behind her. She said, "Child, we don't usually dry mop the bathrooms," and turned and walked out. The girl went back to the hall and began to do the floor. The student expression for not working your job was "frogging". I don't know what it meant, but I didn't want it attached to my name.

Sometime later, I was assigned the job of waiting tables. This was exciting for me, to meet some of the guests and hear tidbits of their conversations. When school started, the dining hall was filled.

After working all summer, I settled in with college classes. In high school, classes were at the Ford Buildings or possibly the Log Cabin Campus. However, college classes were scheduled for the main campus and classes now included boys and girls—a big change from an all boys or all girls school. There was a small library at the Ford Building and I had read all the travel books offered there—from The Bobbsey Twins by Laura Lee Hope to This Good Earth by Pearl S. Buck. There were many more choices at the College Library.

Meals for the girls were still at the Ford Building Dining Hall. However, the boys were served at the Blackstone Dining Hall on the College Campus. There was never any problem getting enough exercise.

There were two literary society groups in college just as there had been in high school. Regular meetings and other activities gave us plenty to do. Sunday School was held at the girls school on Sunday mornings and church was on the college campus. We were "invited" and **expected** to attend. However, the evening attendance for the services held at Barnwell Chapel was on a volunteer basis.

The Bible and the study of the Bible were important parts of the curriculum in high school and college. The requirement was two courses of Bible and/or related subjects.

Music was another important part of the curriculum and life on the Berry Campus. My first experience as a choir member started even before my first class in high school. Miss Warden was in her studio behind the clock tower where she spent her full time in music activities.

There was a staff member, Maurice King, who led the concert choir of boys and girls and the Berry Band, which was boys only. There were several other music groups—chapel choir, quartets, and ensembles.

Miss Warden did not always think very highly of the young men in the concert choir, but she was always at the Grand Piano in the big chapel to accompany the joint choirs in rehearsing "Handel's Messiah".

Maurice King had a child about six or seven years old. As we practiced "Handel's Messiah", there was a commotion at the far end of the row. The little girl had been sitting with a choir member, but she was making her way down the row whispering in each member's ear. When she finally reached me, she pulled my head down close and out loud for everyone to hear she said, "Can YOU take me to the bathroom?" That stopped practice and brought more than a few snickers. Mr. King said, "Hef, let's take that child to the bathroom?" So, we started off to the bathroom.

Joint Chapel was attended by such guests as Henry Ford and Miss Martha Berry. As long as she was able, Miss Berry sat in the upper center front row in the balcony and the choir sang behind her. This was the last place I saw Miss Berry alive.

A Taste of the Real World

After three years of college, I decided I needed to work in the real work place. The railroad was still going down and the money being sent from home was needed at home.

Velma was now working for Farm Security in Dallas, Georgia. Farm Security was doing a lot of work in Paulding County trying to educate and encourage farmers to begin growing and selling chickens—broilers in particular. It was not as successful in Paulding County as in some other counties.

Velma's roommate, Kathleen Weldon, knew a lady in Atlanta who kept boarders. Meals were included and dinner was at 6:00 pm. Ruby, the cook, was a very good cook and tried hard to please the ten or twelve boarders. Her church was having a special week of services and she begged us to go. A car load of us decided to go. Just as the service started, one of the usherettes came to one in our group and asked her to put out her gum. She was terribly embarrassed. Some time later, I went to her home church. I can't remember if she chewed gum there or not, but she was always chewing gum.

Opportunity for Work Experience

I applied for a job in the accounting department of Southern Bell and was given an appointment for an interview. "Romie", who had grown up south of Atlanta, went with me. Velma and Weldon helped me get some "non-Berry" clothes for the interview. The lady who interviewed me looked at my application and then laid it on her desk. She looked at me and said, "You couldn't have done much school. You were into too many other activities." I just smiled but made no comment. I got a job in the Toll Accounts Department. Bills had to be sorted, posted, and calculated by different people. After the bill was calculated, there were other people, checkers, to recheck each bill. If a bill got through to the customer and it had been calculated incorrectly, it was not the checker who was blamed, but the one who had calculated it. I always thought that was a bit unfair . . . . Shouldn't it have been a "shared error"?

Another thing I did not like and which confused me for a time—if Southern Bell was shorthanded and we got to, or perhaps had to work overtime, our checks were almost smaller than those with no overtime at all because of the taxes withheld on the larger check amount. It was almost like paying to work for Southern Bell.

Before I began working at Southern Bell, I told my supervisor I would be going back to school in the fall. However, like the Dean at Berry College, they did not act like they believed me. They sent me to a business school to learn more about their machines.

Mulinix, my name for Rufus Eugene Mulinix, had started to Berry College on a work scholarship. He drove the Laundry Truck, collecting the laundry and delivering it to the Laundry Room in the lower floor of the girl's dorm. No one asked him if he had a license when he was assigned to the job. Most of his route was off the public highway, but there was a short stretch where he had to get on the public road. One day he was stopped. I don't remember what happened, but shortly after that, Roland, my cousin, talked Mulinix into joining the service with him.

About the time I was sent to school by Southern Bell, Mulinix was also sent to school to learn Morse Code in training for Radio Operator. It was a part of Reconnaissance Training. He was in school on December 7, 1941, when Pearl Harbor was bombed. Everything tightened up after Pearl Harbor.

Return to School

When I did return to Berry, I went to the Dean's office and said, "I'm Ba-ack." She was surprised to see me. She really did not believe I would come back. We began working to set up my schedule. **Problem**: I had never been classified as a senior. Each grade had a different color dress and to get my green senior dress I had to be classified a senior. I did not have enough credit hours. You had to be within two quarters of graduating. Taking the time away from school to work left me just short of what I needed.

I had not done any "Practice Teaching" and decided if I could get it, that was what I wanted to do. They set me up to teach Social Studies to the new work scholarship girls after supper. I had barely gotten started when I was called to the office. They needed an English Teacher for the tenth grade. They told me if I would do the English class, I would have enough credit hours for my Professional Teacher Certificate. So I began teaching tenth grade English.

One of the perks of being a senior was not being required to go to breakfast. As the new English Teacher, I had to give up this cherished perk. The class was the first thing in the morning. When the class ended, I expected to receive the Professional Teacher Certificate as promised. However, I was told I could not receive the Professional Teacher Certificate and would only receive a Provisional Certificate. The reason—too many courses at one time!

In preparation for graduation we all needed black shoes. I did not have any black shoes. It was war time; leather items were hard to come by. It was customary for college seniors to act as escorts to go with under classmen to shop in Rome. Ordinarily we had to check out at the office, hire a taxi and go to Rome to do our shopping. Each time I went to escort other students shopping I was looking for black shoes to wear with my cap and gown. On one trip I found a pair of shoes which really looked more like house shoes. I bought a pair. When I tried them on back on campus I realized that they were not leather. We had to go to the Big Chapel on the lower campus for the Baccalaureate service. It was a rainy day. By the time I got back to the dormitory, the shoes were soaked. I set them aside to dry. I wore them to graduation and someone said to me, "Your shoes are coming apart." I looked down and with every step I took I left a part of my shoes behind. We went on through the service. As they came apart, they became bigger and bigger. I remember crossing the platform to receive my diploma and the snickers at the way I was walking with my big loose, falling apart shoes.

After graduation one of my fellow students came up to me and said, "Now Hef, you have your diploma. Where's your Wedding certificate?" I told them "I don't have a Wedding Certificate." I had sent it to Mr. Ben but I did not admit that to anyone at that time. Mother and Velma had come to graduation. Velma had a new car. They helped me pack, carried me to the Train station and helped get my train pass. Then I was on my way to Meridian, Mississippi.

Chapter Six

A BRAVE NEW WORLD

Rufus Eugene Mulinix and I were secretly married in December, 1943, before graduation. It had to be kept secret or I would have been expelled. During the Christmas break from school, I took a train to Meridian, Mississippi to meet Mulinix. He had made all the arrangements he could. The bride and groom were required to sign a ledger at the courthouse. When I told the lady my age, 21, the lady said, "Honey, in this state you don't have to be 21 to get married. So, let's put your correct age." I really was 21.

Having met the requirements of the state of Mississippi, we went to the Base Chapel and walked through the ceremony with the chaplain. The chapel was decorated very nicely by a Woman's Club in Meridian. There was a great big Christmas tree in the corner. Afterward, we went to the commissary and ate a banana split. Then Mulinix took me to the hotel where he had made reservations for an extended stay. He had to return to the base.

The next day, December 22, 1943, we were married. When the Chaplain came to the part in the ceremony about the rings, he asked for the ring and we just looked at him and shook our heads, "No." It was in Mulinix's pocket, but we didn't want the ceremony to be about the ring, but about the vows we had made to each other. I did not wear the wedding ring until after graduation.

Many of the men in Mulinix's company were upset because he had planned the wedding during their work schedule and they were unable to attend. The only people at the wedding were men from the Radio Operator group, his best friend on the base and his wife who stood up with us, and the Post photographer who made a few pictures. When we started back to the hotel, the men teased Mulinix and he made a gesture that said, "I'm going this way. Where are you going?" which actually meant, "See you later."

We ate at the base and I got sick on something. We walked and talked and watched the time very closely. I had to take the train to

Birmingham then change trains to get back to school. My roommate, Romell Stallings, met my train and we took a taxi to Berry and back to life on the college campus.

Whenever Mulinix was able to get a leave, he would call the Dean and ask for permission to call on me. The first time it happened, I was in my room and Miss Alston called me to her office. When I arrived, she said, "Do you have plans for Sunday?" I said "Ma'am?" "Do you have plans for Sunday afternoon? I have made a date for you." she announced.

"What?!" I asked, stunned. She knew Mulinix and I had been keeping steady company. How could she? She wouldn't . . . My mind was racing. "Just be at your usual meeting place Sunday afternoon," she said with a big smile. I knew who my date was, and I could hardly wait.

Visitation was supposed to be limited to once a month, but Mulinix was stationed in Atlanta and came every weekend. (I believe Dean Alston was sympathetic to our situation, since she lost her love in the war.) Anyway, the Dean would see me and call out "Hef! I suppose you have no plans for Sunday afternoon." I would reply, "No." I knew Mulinix would be there soon.

One day I made a trip to Rome on behalf of the Annual Staff soliciting ads for publication in the Annual. I had not taken any one with me. I had taken a taxi into Rome. When I came out of my first appointment there was Mulinix. He said that we were going for a ride. I felt that I was on thin ice for going somewhere without telling the office at Berry, but he insisted. Before long we were in a rural section of Bartow County. He pulled under two large oak trees that shaded the Mulinix home place. I found out I was to meet his family. We just sat in the car until Mr. Ben came over with his hunting dogs. These dogs seemed shy and docile around Mr. Ben, however, they would have nothing to do with me. Mr. Ben began to talk softly to them telling them "She is going to be part of the family now. She will be good to you. She is coming to live with us and we will all love her." He pulled the dogs up to him, one on each side. As he continued to talk softly, the dogs snuggled closer and actually laid their heads against him like they were embracing him with rumbling sounds and tails wagging as if to say "Okay, we'll accept her. It's okay." Mr. Ben broke the contact by saying "Okay fellows, Gene wants to show her the rest of the yard. I was impressed by this introduction, especially when Mulinix spread both arms and gathered the dogs to him and said, "This is home, isn't it?" The dogs and I became friends, especially around feeding time. Later, I was introduced to the rest of Mulinix's family.

By this time, everyone knew we were a couple. On the night before graduation, there was a reception to honor the graduates. I happened to be sitting next to the Dean. She leaned over and said, "Hef, I've heard a rumor that you are married." I replied, "You know Miss Alston, I've been hearing the same rumor." Just at that moment a gentlemen asked me to dance. All the guys were told, "When she starts talking about 'Sarge', you know you are dancing too close." They all knew us, seemed to like us, and wished us well.

Uneasy Moments

I had kept our Marriage Certificate. I got a little uneasy thinking it might be discovered in a room check. I always knew the mail could be censored. So I gathered up my marriage certificate and sent it to Mr. Ben, Mulinix's father. I told him to give it to Eugene when he saw him. I walked to the main post office so it would not go through the girl's school mail.

Mr. Ben lived alone at 100 Mulinix Road. Mulinix's sister, Sara Lou, would come spend the day and do the cooking and cleaning. The day the letter came, Sara Lou was there. This was the first she knew about our marriage—she was not too happy.

I always seemed to room with Home Economic majors. I learned a lot of things from them. I worked with my roommate, Nancy Moore, to help her meet the outside reading requirements and she gave me a copy of the cook book that was standard requirement for all Home Economic majors—<u>The American Woman's Cook Book</u>. It has been a great help throughout my life. Fifty years later, my "old green cook book" was in shreds. With Victor's help, we located and purchased online, a copy of the "old green cook book" for each of the grandsons for Christmas. The prices varied. The most we paid for a cook book was $51.00. Some of them were less than $25.00. We planned for each gift to be about $50.00. If the book didn't cost $50.00, they were given the change up to $50.00. The oldest grandson got to pick first. The second could take his book or pick another. They had great fun swapping and finally keeping their own cook book. It was so popular we ordered one for Gene, Victor, and one to stay with me—the $51.00 one. I still have it.

On May 22, 1944, I received my Bachelor of Science degree from Berry College at the big chapel. After graduation, and a change of shoes, my mother and Velma helped me pack and took me to the train station. They helped get my ticket on the afternoon train and sent me on my way to Meridian, Mississippi and Mulinix.

I didn't sleep much on the train—too excited I guess. When the train arrived in Meridian, there were ten to fifteen men running alongside the train yelling, "We're going to Augusta! We're going to Augusta!" The base was actually in Aiken, South Carolina just outside of Augusta. The conductor escorted me to the exit door where I had to hug my way to Mulinix through every service man between me and him. He was in the very back of the crowd. He kidded me for a long time about me hugging everybody before he got a hug.

Mulinix had been paying rent on an apartment for about a month. However, we didn't go there right away. Everyone went to the boarding house for breakfast. I was beat and fell asleep at the table.

Ann, the wife of one of the other servicemen, took charge and told everybody to leave or go to another room quietly. She was putting me to bed. I slept most of the day. When I woke up Mulinix was there and he took me to the apartment. He couldn't stay. He had to get back to the base.

When the day came to leave, we boarded the troop train to Augusta. We traveled all day and all night. By morning, as we were arriving, there were others who were leaving. So, when we began looking for lodging, a room had just opened up at a boarding house run by an elderly couple. There were three couples living in the house.

Marking Time

During the day, I was alone and on my own. I would go to the drugstore snack bar for lunch. I kept two or three books for reading. I had fabric cut out that I carried around until I found a sewing machine and had a chance to sew. One evening when Mulinix came home, we went to a small restaurant and ordered chicken. When it came, it was almost raw and we got sick from it. From then on, the landlord saw to it that we had something to eat. She began to include me in her daily activities. I stayed there until Mulinix shipped out to Florida.

It was at this time that Mulinix came down with the mumps. He thought at first, it was a wisdom tooth giving him trouble. But the Army doctor told him it was the mumps and that I would probably get them too, unless I had already had them. Sure enough, by the end of the incubation period, I also had the mumps.

Cross City

When we arrived in Florida, we lived in a "shotgun" house—really just barracks put up quickly for military men and their families. There were two rooms and a common room used by everyone for cooking. For three months, I read books, finally began to sew, and finished my garment. When Mulinix was home, we would walk on the beach, collect seashells, driftwood, and other memorabilia. On rare occasions we would take short outings to places like Cypress Gardens to watch the water show. It was on one of these outings that I got severely sunburned. The doctor told Mulinix he should send me home. I was not used to the hot Florida climate. He didn't realize "home" was only 100-150 miles from there.

During this time I became pregnant. When the training mission ended, Mulinix had some leave time so we took a trip to 100 Mulinix Road to see his family and give them our news. After a short stay, we went on to Millen and I stayed as Mulinix was being sent overseas.

The Troop train left from Augusta west to California, where they boarded a ship. They zigzagged across the Pacific and finally ended up on the East Coast of India.

In India, Mulinix and a group of men were living off base. His group was responsible for the information they were getting about terrain and troop movements in China and beyond. This was recon work, where they took photographs as well as personal observation One of their responsibilities was to recover any aircraft that had crashed before returning to base. Mulinix's group transmitted all their messages in code to headquarters. His group would do things together. He had some interesting photographs. When near the Taj Mahal, they could not get on the property, but they could fly around it. They did and took pictures.

They watched farmers work all day in the flooded rice fields, At the end of the day they bathed with their clothes on, washed the cattle, then dipped a bucket of water to take home and use in their cooking. The natives wore their clothes until they were filthy then they just threw them away instead of washing their cloths. They lived a very primitive life.

As the war with Japan came to a end, they again boarded a funny little train to the west coast of India. They took a boat through the Red Sea and the Suez Canal into the Mediterranean Sea, and finally back to New York. From New York they traveled back to the base in South Carolina where they were discharged. They had traversed around the globe. Mulinix took another train ride, eventually arriving in Kingston, Ga. and 100 Mulinix Road.

CHAPTER SEVEN

HOME AGAIN ON BARTON HILL

My parents had once again moved into an Apprentice Foreman's house in Millen with only one bedroom. There was really no room for me. Daddy John was away with his Extra Gang, so Mother and I decided to move into the house on the Barton Place, since they still owned it. We packed as much as we could into the car and moved back to the Barton Hill house.

New Life

Mr. Reeves was a good neighbor. He was always watching over us when Daddy John was gone. On March 15th or 16th, he came over to check on me. There was a dark storm cloud overhead and he said, "This cloud is a good time for having a baby." I told him there were no signs of anything yet.

The next morning, Daddy John was home and took me to the doctor. I still was not doing anything. The doctor induced labor and on March 17, 1945 my first son, Gene, was born. He was a healthy, bouncing boy. However, I developed a very high fever and nausea. I couldn't eat. I stayed in the hospital for about two or three weeks. As quickly as the fever came, it left. Dr. Cleveland Thompson said he had given me his whole month's allotment of penicillin. I went home, but it was short lived. I ate something before leaving the hospital and by the time I reached home I began vomiting again. Back to the hospital—Dr. Thompson began asking me questions. "What did you eat before you left?" I ate some turnip greens," I replied. "Why did you eat that?" he barked. "I thought I had to so I could go home," I cried.

Gene began crying. Mother was carrying him around on a pillow. She handed him to me and we both stayed in the hospital another two or three days. Finally, Dr. Thompson transferred me to the hospital in Waynesboro under Dr. Miller Byrne. He told him, "I've done all I know for this child. I don't know what it was but we've come through it." When I woke up, they were at the foot of my bed discussing a fishing trip!

Finally—home to stay. The first thing I saw as we pulled in the yard was a line full of diapers—"the flags of every nation" is what Mrs. Minnie Lester called them. The doctor told my daddy, "You tell that young man, this little lady is not to have any more babies." Daddy told Mother; Mother told me; I told Mulinix; and we both said, "Pooh."

Before my baby was born, I had wanted to get a baby bed. Mother wouldn't let me. She said, "If anything were to happen, we wouldn't want a baby bed around that we could not use."

Although I saw Dr. Thompson on occasion, Dr. Byrne began giving me all kinds of tests. In one test, I was to eat two slices of white bread before coming to the hospital. I would always leave the baby with mother and Jo would drive me to the drugstore snack bar across the street from the doctor's office. She would have me eat my two pieces of bread like a sandwich. We would wait about fifteen minutes and go to the hospital. When I got there, he pumped my stomach to see what was happening. He would wait five minutes and pump my stomach again. He found the digestive juices were there—just not functioning as they should. After he finished the test, he sent me back to the snack bar to have a chicken sandwich. Then we went home.

Velma's Wedding

When Gene was about three months old, Velma decided on a date for her wedding. She wanted to be married in the house. She wanted everything in the wedding to be a part of our "stuff". We didn't have a punch bowl, so Mother and I got the Sears Roebuck Catalog down. We found one and purchased it. I still have it today. I tried several times to give it to Velma, but she had no use for it. She married Mike Finch of Dallas, GA. He ran a mill that ground corn, wheat and other grains. He then sold it to the farmers in the area.

Mrs. Waters decorated the house. She was the wife of one of the railroad bosses. We had known her since our Mogul days. They had a car with two sets of wheels—one for the road and one for the rails.

The wedding was for the family mainly, because the house was so small. I was supposed to serve the punch at the reception. I had gotten a young girl to watch the baby and I told her if he got fussy or started to cry to take him outside. As I served the punch, who should show up in the line but this young girl? I asked, "Where's my baby?" She said, "Oh, Mrs. Velma has him." I looked around and sure enough, Velma had him showing him to everybody she came in contact with. He was just another one of her "Dollies".

Chapter Eight

OUR REAL HOME AT LAST

Mr. Ben and his wife, Iva L. Fields Mulinix, had moved to 100 Mulinix Road and rented the property from Mrs. Emma Sheets in 1925. She had acquired the land when the bank in Kingston failed. It was a "Rent to Own" deal. Mr. Ben gathered vegetables every day for home and for sale in Kingston and Rome, as well as for the Sheets family, where he would put the vegetables in their refrigerator and just leave. In 1944, the balance was "Paid in Full". They had four children. Joe Ben was the oldest, Sara Lou was second, Rufus Eugene "Mulinix" was third, and Bill was the youngest.

In World War I, I believe, all five sons of the Sullivan family joined the service or were drafted in the same war. One by one, all five sons were killed in the war. As a result, a law was passed that said not all sons could be drafted or serve at the same time. One must be left at home. The government was not supposed to take all of Mr. Ben's boys. Mr. Ben was working to get Bill discharged when he received notification that in August, Bill had been killed in France.

When Gene was about five months old, I was still under a doctor's care. Mr. Ben wanted to see his grandson, but he was waiting to hear from Mulinix and didn't want to leave. He wanted us to come to him. Joe Ben and Louise Russell had gotten married and were already there. Boot and Sara Lou were also there. The doctor told me, "I will agree for you to go, if you will check in with my friend, Dr. William Harbin."

Gene and I took the first available train to Atlanta where Velma picked us up and brought us to 100 Mulinix Road. Mr. Ben had heard that Mulinix had arrived in New York and was waiting on his discharge papers. It could take five to fifteen days.

Mr. Ayler Gallagher, who was a supervisor with the railroad, was at the railroad station when a telegram came in saying Mulinix would arrive on the early train the next day. He took a copy of the telegram to Mr. Ben. "If he comes in on the 7 o'clock," Mr.

Gallagher said, "I'll bring him right out." Mulinix did, and Mr. Gallagher did. I was still in my blue chenille robe. Mr. Ben was making syrup. I had the baby in my arms and he didn't like this reunion a little bit. The next few days are a blur. It was just a joy being here. Mulinix had leave time that lasted until his discharge papers came through.

With rationing, you couldn't get meat. Every now and then somebody would kill a calf or pig and sell part of it. Pa, Mr. Ben, had gotten a beef roast. Sara Lou put it in a pot with water. I was so-o-o disappointed with the meat—boiled instead of roasted.

As long as he lived, Mr. Ben stayed here with us. He enjoyed hunting as most of the Mulinix men do. There are two rules for hunting: (1) You eat what you kill. (2) If you kill it, you clean it and make it ready for cooking. That put a little meat on the table at a time when meat was scarce in the market place. He always helped as much as he could with everything from cooking breakfast to tending the children, especially Victor. He would make biscuits and when he put them in the oven, he called everyone and expected us to be at the table in three minutes. Mr. Ben did one thing that was so special. On someone's birthday he would turn their plate upside down and underneath would be a one dollar bill. He also did this at Christmas for everyone. All the plates were upside down and a dollar bill was under each one.

Joe Ben came home before Mulinix and had started working on the bridge gang under Mr. Gallagher. Mr. Gallagher asked Mulinix if he had a job. Mulinix opened his hand and said, "Here's my job."

By the end of 1946, Joe Ben and Louise had moved out. Boot and Sara Lou had also moved out, and I was pregnant again. I checked in with Dr. Bill Harbin. Within three months, we learned that Sara Lou was also with child. We were both under Dr. Bill Harbin's care. He decided to give up his obstetric practice and go into surgery. The date of his last delivery would be the end of September, 1947. Victor was born September 4, 1947. Sara Lou's baby was born in December. She was very upset at me and Dr. Harbin, because I was a new patient and he delivered my baby, Victor. She had been his patient longer but he did not deliver her baby. Of course, it wasn't my fault. But that didn't make a difference with Sara Lou.

As a baby, Victor had one eye that didn't follow. When people noticed it, they would say, "Oh, he'll grow out of it." But there was one lady, Lillian, a tenant farmer, who as a child had a roving eye. She told me, "Don't listen to them. I can remember when I could see out of both eyes. Now I can only see out of one. You have to get him some help as soon as you can."

We called around and found the visit and examination would be $25.00. He was diagnosed with Monocular Vision—seeing with only one eye at a time. My daddy paid for the first visit—the first of many. By the time he was eighteen months old he was wearing glasses and had regular visits to the eye doctor. At $25.00 a visit, it soon became a strain on the budget.

In 1947, Mr. Ben deeded the farm to his children. Mulinix received the land on the east side of the road and Joe Ben and Sara Lou received that on the west side of the road. Our first tax bill on the property was in 1948 in the amount of $27.30.

Mulinix tried long and hard to make a go of the farm. He attended the Farm School the government offered to veterans to learn ways to help make his farming more productive. He was introduced to many different things. He tried a variety of them—raising hogs, chickens, both broilers and laying hens, and rabbits. He thought he needed more land for all these animals and to raise cotton, vegetables, and some fruits. He rented the adjacent land and signed a contract with Pamona Products in 1949 to raise Pimento peppers.

The peppers were carefully graded, and of course, there were some culls. Mulinix came up with the idea of feeding the culls to the laying hens. It seemed to be working fine. The hens liked the peppers. The customers, however, complained about the bright red yolks in the eggs.

From the farm, the peppers were taken to Cartersville, where they were picked up by truck and taken to the processing plant in Griffin, Georgia.

Some of the veterans pooled their money and purchased a much better breeding boar. Studies had shown they could produce more piglets and better, sturdier piglets. They named the boar, Solomon. When it came time for a sow to be serviced, they just backed the trailer they had made up to his pen and he almost ran into it. It was as though he knew he was "going visiting".

One day Mr. Ben was watching a sow with several piglets tagging along, go into the field to graze on a thick patch of clover. All went well until the mama rubbed against the electric fence designed to keep the hogs corralled. It didn't seem to hurt the mama, but those squealing little piglets went everywhere. Mr. Ben doubled over with laughter while the baby pigs tried to find their right place and the mama just continued to enjoy the lush clover.

One of Mr. Ben's renters had a new baby. She also had a four year old. One day as I was washing outside, I picked up a pair of the little boy's overalls and put them in the washing. When I tried to put them through the ringer, they would not go. When I got to searching through the pockets, I found a broken egg shell and a perfectly formed baby chick in the bib pocket. It was dead of course, and I believe Pa and the little boy buried it.

Beyond Farming

Finally, the decision was made for me to try to begin teaching. Mr. Ben agreed to watch the boys. Mulinix would get a job, also. We had heard that Lemuel Tankerlsey was Principal in Adairsville. We had known him for some time. On Sunday afternoon, we started toward Adairsville to see him. On the way we met a man who flagged us down. It turned out to be Mr. White from the Adairsville School System. "We heard you were trained as a teacher," he began, "We wondered if you would be interested in coming to Adairsville." We said, "Yes. We were just on our way to see the principal there to see if he had any positions available." "Yes, yes," he said. He has three positions available."

So we went on to Adairsville. **Problem:** It had been five years since I had received my teaching certificate and it had expired.

Things never seemed to come easy. But as luck would have it, Bub Sheets, principal of Kingston Elementary, and a Georgia Tech graduate, and Mrs. Molly Bell Vincent were planning to go to Berry to get their certificates renewed. So I tagged along. Bub drove and it was not the smoothest ride. He used his gas to go up a hill. At the top of the hill, he turned his motor off and coasted down the hill to conserve gas. One morning we were about a minute late meeting Bub and we saw Bub's car disappear around the curve. Mulinix had to take me. When we got there Mulinix told Bub, "Don't you leave her. You left her this morning." We were told if we went to Atlanta we could get our certificates much sooner than trying to do them in the mail. There was some irregularity in Mrs. Vincent's college credits but the attendant told her he could overlook it for one, but not the other two. Of course, there were no irregularities in ours, so no problem.

I took a required subject, "Test and Measurement" to get my certificate—this time the Professional Teacher Certificate. Again, the class was designed toward seniors. It was actually the introduction to standardized testing and counseling. It was being pushed for all high schools and some middle schools.

Before I could start school, I needed some dresses. Mulinix had a lot of feed sacks which had some very nice prints on them. Mother was able to make me several dresses for school. A short time later, Daddy John was transferred to Machen and they moved to Shadydale, GA.

Cotton dresses have to be ironed. The only iron I had needed to be heated on the wood stove or on the hearth of the fireplace. About every two weeks, we visited Shadydale with my clothes washed and sprinkled down ready to be ironed while Daddy enjoyed the boys. There was never any problem getting help with the ironing or watching the children. The wives of Daddy John's railroad crew always wanted to work for "Caps" missus.

With my new dresses, I began my teaching career in Bartow County in the '49-'50 school year in Adairsville. There were three positions available: sixth grade, Librarian, and Shop/Agriculture. My certificate did not qualify me for Librarian or the Shop/Agriculture. There was a young couple, Alvin and Julia Witherington, who had just graduated and wanted very much to be hired for the other positions. I was assigned to the sixth grade class and classroom by the established sixth grade teacher, who divided the children into "Group A" and "Group B". I was given "Group A", the ones the established teacher knew all too well.

When I was shown to my classroom, it looked more like a storeroom. There were two primitive tables, maybe a half-dozen desks, no teacher's desk, nor storage space for teaching materials. As the students arrived, they were good sports and helped me find seats for everybody—stools, chairs, and even some Coca Cola crates. To get to the classroom, you had to go up two flights of steps. There were three doors—one for Home Economics, one for a Business Class, and one was an informal storeroom—my room.

When school had been in session for about ten days to two weeks, there was a loud banging on my door. I went to the door and there stood a little man with glasses down on his nose. There was no introduction, or preliminary "Hello". He said, "I want your register." I had been told that my register did not leave my hands. I was not to give it to anyone. I replied, "What!" He repeated impatiently, "I want your register." I replied, "I'm sorry. You can't have my register. You may come in and look at it, but you can't take it out."

The man stomped out of the room and went to the principal's office, to Mr. Lemuel Tankersley. He began with great frustration, "That **child** you have out there won't give me her register!" Mr. Tankersley replied, "Did you introduce yourself?" "No!" he continued, "Everybody knows who I am."

"Well, that 'child' as you call her, has no reason to know you. It's her first year to teach. Let's go back there and I will introduce you and I think you will find she is very cooperative."

When Mr. Tankersley introduced Dr. Lance from the State Department of Education and explained his purpose for asking for the register, I apologized saying, "I'm very sorry. I did not know who you were. If I had known, of course, I would have given you my register."

Dr. Lance was at a loss for words, but finally got out an apology for not introducing himself. The next week, there were thirty brand new student desks in my classroom.

Years later, I was invited to join the Delta Kappa Gamma Society, an honor for any school teacher. I was introduced to a very dignified, very beautiful elderly lady, and honorary member of the Society. When she heard my name she said, "Oh Honey, I know who you are. You're the one that Lance was so rude to." I just chuckled and said, "Oh, it was just a little misunderstanding."

It was in 1979 that we began our annual Thanksgiving trip to Aunt Florence's. We would go out to eat. When she could no longer hear well enough to carry on a conversation, or see well enough to read the menu, it was no longer fun. Mary Elizabeth and I started cooking Thanksgiving dinner and taking it to them. They would come to the back door when they saw us pull in the driveway. Aunt Florence always wanted things put back where she left them and done the way she had always done them.

Each fall, while we were in Kentucky with the Campbells, Victor, Marty, and Ben would come to the farm and enjoy their time off by raking leaves and cleaning the yard. Today, the yard has fewer trees. We seem to lose one now and then. So, now there are fewer leaves to rake.

After my first year teaching sixth grade in Adairsville, a sixth grade class came open in Kingston Elementary School. I changed schools.

It was at this time that I began to teach GAs at Kingston Baptist Church. We met at my house and we had fun. One of the programs we presented to the church was the Queen's Ceremony, the highest step for our girls. Scripture memorization was one of the steps required on their way to becoming Queen.

When we presented the program, the pastor came up to me and said, "They always told me they had fun. I just figured they didn't do much but play around. But they had fun and still turned out THIS?!"

The girls thought Mother was their personal seamstress with the little costumes Mother and I put together for them. This same group of girls, when I went to Cassville High School, asked Mr. Dickey if they could have a Tri-Hi-Y Club. Mr. Dickey told them, "I'd be glad for you to have a club, but I have not been able to get a leader." To which they responded excitedly, "If we can find a leader, can we start a Tri-Hi-Y Club?" "Sure," he replied. Mr. Dickey didn't know they had already talked with me. For the last two years I was at Cass High, we had a pretty successful Club. The Hi-Y for the boys was started as well, but never seemed as active as the Tri-Hi-Y.

I taught five years in Kingston. In the 1951-1952 school year, my son, Gene, started to school. They moved from the historical brick building to the new brick building—NO MORE POTBELLIED STOVES! The Army Surplus barracks were removed from the property. Things were looking up—at home as well. For the first time we had electricity. Of course, we had to do some remodeling of the house to accommodate an electric stove and refrigerator, which replaced the Kerosene appliances. We purchased a new '51Chevrolet with a monthly payment of approximately $68.00.

At the beginning of the '53-'54 school year, Victor, my second son, started to school. In October, I had to take leave time from my job, to have my tonsils removed. Mulinix had just begun a job with Cleveland Electric, and my "Daddy John" died. He is buried in the Annex part of Oakland Cemetery in Rome, GA.

Cleveland Electric Company had a contract to construct the GE plant in Rome. Mulinix was involved with the installation of the electric wiring in that big complex. He met a man in the personnel department who knew Mr. Ben. They talked off and on and he suggested Mulinix should apply for a job with GE. He did and when the plant opened, he began working with GE.

In 1954, I began to collect Pottery little by little and Victor was still having regular eye check ups with Dr. Tom Harbin, who said more than once, "If I had more patients like Victor, I'd take down my shingle." It was so frustrating—not only for him but for Victor as well. He continued to work with Victor's eyes, but Victor was also having trouble with his speech. Dr. Harbin referred us to The Rome, GA. Junior League Speech School and Carolyn Floyd, a speech therapist with the Junior League, to help Victor learn to speak more clearly.

In one session she was trying to get Victor to say his "sh" sound. She asked him," What does your daddy do every morning?" To which Victor replied, "I don't know." She drew a picture of a window shade and asked, "What is that?" To which Victor replied, "I don't know." When she told him it was a window shade, he said, "Oh, my grandmother has some of those." Finally, she directed him to say "shoes and socks". To which Victor replied, "Dos and docks."

Not all sessions were as difficult or frustrating as this one. With patience and persistent coaching, he learned how to breathe and form his words. Today, you would never know he had ever had a problem.

In 1955, we purchased our first freezer—a Bendix 18 ½ ft. freezer. We also installed Butane gas to supplement the wood burning heat. We took Gene to the orthodontist. While still in high school, Mulinix began losing his teeth. By the time he came home from the service, he had a full set of dentures. My teeth were uneven, but good. We felt it was important to take care of Gene's teeth which were also uneven.

Gene always wanted a piano. So we bought one from one of Mulinix's cousins. We made arrangements with Mrs. Nelle Rollins for piano lessons. Gene took a few lessons and shortly lost interest and gave up practice and lessons. He sang in the Cartersville High School Chorus, but never mastered the piano. Victor followed in his brother's footsteps—he quit piano—but today he sings in the Kingston Church Choir which his wife directs.

In May, 1956, after my fifth year at Kingston, health issues caused me to take time off from work outside the home. Mulinix was now working at GE in Rome and still trying to work the farm. We determined that we would be able to manage on what we had at the farm and his salary. We purchased an 18 ft Maytag freezer and a cherry bedroom suite. We still use the bedroom suite it in our bedroom.

In 1957 we got some rabbits, a new station wagon, and Ed Dickey approached me about teaching at Cassville High School. My subject was to be eleventh grade English Grammar and American Literature with one semester of English Grammar and one semester of American Literature, my special area of interest. At first, I said, "No." But rethinking it, and realizing that the problem with my son's eyes was not going away, I decided to try it. I put on my Sunday best dress and went for the interview with Ed Dickey. The conversation during the interview went something like this:

Ed Dickey: "You are mighty little."

Martha: "Been little all my life."

Ed Dickey: "These are big boys. I don't know if you can handle them."

Martha: "I handled some pretty large sixth grade boys."

Ed Dickey decided to let me try.

In my enthusiasm to bond with my students, I made a sign for an upcoming football game. When I finished it, I was pleased with it and waited for my students. One of the students in my freshman homeroom came up to me and said, "Teach, you did a real good job on the sign, but you have the colors reversed!"

They always called me "Teach". I remember a student at Kingston school who was always causing or trying to cause problems. Once, late in the day, we were relaxed, or tired, and he said, "Teach, you must have been the meanest kid in your school." "Why's that?" I asked. "'Cause, you know all the tricks." he replied.

One day, I was expounding on a piece of poetry about spring in American Literature. After class, one of my students made the remark, "I have been in churches where they opened the doors of the church and they that were not as convincing as you were."

I began to realize that these students had never done anything. They had never performed in a one-act play. They had never done any memorization. Nothing! As one of the junior sponsors, along with Mr. Roberts and Ms. Pullam, our duties included planning and putting on the Junior-Senior Prom. The gym was the customary site for the Prom and the juniors were responsible for furnishing the entertainment and refreshment.

In our area, there were certain contests in music, recitation, and drama, or one-act plays. I began to urge students to choose one literary event and be involved in it. One of my students, Barbara Bennett, took it to heart. She won third place in an essay contest sponsored by the Cartersville Civitan Club in 1961.

We started a drama unit. The Librarian helped choose some drama reference books. In the meantime, I searched for one-act plays for thirty students and planned for each junior homeroom to plan one. These were not for contests but a fundraiser for the Junior-Senior Prom.

Using what they had learned, the students made lists of their needs, from the director to the prop manager. They finally chose three one-act plays—almost slapstick comedy. One that comes to mind was set in a doctor's office. In the opening scene, Nellie Harris with her two boys and a girl trailing behind, comes into the office and plops down on the seat and says, "Don't it feel good to "set" down?" fanning herself with both hands.

Prompters, lighting people, publicity, ticket sales—everybody was involved. The director was assigned to take a copy of the play and insert a page with items needed, or direction for costumes and lighting, and for placing everything for everyone at the time and place needed.

Mr. Roberts, the Agriculture and Shop teacher, took the boys and put up lights and a curtain. They helped obtain furnishings. We borrowed the sofa from the Home Economics Department and in the process of moving it, one of the legs was broken. We had to have it repaired and we paid for it out of the proceeds.

The students learned to reference the instructions so anyone could understand them. Each student was responsible for two tickets—one of which was for themselves. We wanted to insure some kind of audience. I made sure, by hook or by crook, that every student got their tickets. Not all could afford them. The plays went over with a bang. The students enjoyed it the most.

When I asked Bill Kimes, the Senior Representative how much money he thought we would need, he replied, "Every penny you can raise and $10.00 more." A little perturbed, I said, "You're no help." and I walked away.

The next year we decided to do something for the school. We purchased five books for the Library and presented them to Miss Louise Ward, the Librarian.

The following year, 1959-'60, I had noticed there were no dictionaries anywhere except one or two in the Library. I contacted the person who purchased books for the school. We bought thirty dictionaries and put them in the desks in my room. Anyone could use them, but they had to sign them out to take them home. After I left, the dictionaries were distributed into the other rooms.

Early on, the Curriculum Director for the County, Blanche Carver, began urging me to take advantage of the scholarships and/or loans aimed toward an Advanced degree in Guidance and Counseling. From then until I quit working, that was my focus. I moved from Adairsville Elementary, to Kingston Elementary School to Cass High, to the Cartersville City School System with activities and assignments at Junior High, and High School, as well as system wide duties.

Blanche Carver helped me enroll in the University of Georgia Masters Program about 1960 while at Cass High. I completed the course and received the Certificate for Specialist in Education in Guidance and Counseling in August, 1967 while I was working in the Cartersville City School System.

For part of the sixth year application, I needed a health certificate or a doctor's signature on a form stating I was healthy enough to take the course. Dr. William Harbin would not sign the form—another roadblock to overcome. I continued with and finished the program, but without the health form I couldn't get credit.

Ed Dickey was still principal at Cass High, but not as satisfied in his job—some sort of dispute with the Board of Education. He received an offer of employment from the Cartersville City School System. He took the job and most of the teachers at Cass High with him. Only two remained of the longtime teachers at Cass High. I was not one of those who stayed. I went to Cartersville.

Our family's schedules were heavy. The boys were both still in school and I was teaching as well as working in the field of counseling and guidance. At the end of the '67-'68 school year, my contract was not renewed and I have not taught in the public school system since. Ironically, the stipulation for a health form was eventually no longer required. I finally received my Specialist in Education Diploma in June, 1971—three years after I had left the Public School System.

Chapter Nine

INTERNATIONAL TRAVEL

By the early 1960's, Mother was making her home with Jo and Oscar and was legally their dependent. Oscar was in the Air Force—the Strategic Air Command. He had been transferred from Oklahoma, to Washington State, and finally to Upper Heyford, England.

When it was clear that Oscar and Jo were going to be stationed in England, I immediately began the process of getting my passport. Mulinix had his from the service.

Before moving to England, they learned that an animal coming over from the States had to be quarantined for one month. So one month before leaving, Oscar and Jo shipped the cat over so it would be ready to come out of quarantine when they arrived. The cat was so glad to see them, he just went "crazy"—jumping, meowing and rubbing up against them.

The cat had free run of the house. The windows had no screens and opened in and out. One morning Oscar was leaving for work. He went out the door, but was back in shortly with the cat. He handed the cat to Jo and said, "Do something with this damn cat!" Jo took him and put him in the pantry. Victor and I think "Damn Cat" was its name. We never heard him called anything else.

One day after returning to the states, the cat went out to lay in the sun. When they began to look for him, they found him on top of a building. He was dead.

Mother was not in the best of health. In fact, Oscar first vetoed the plan to take Mother with them to England. He was afraid she might die over there and they might not be able to get her back home due to some regulations.

In 1966, Mother fell. She was taken to the base hospital. The doctors there sent her on to the Emergency Room in London for further testing and observation. Jo called me and told me she had made my reservation on the first flight to London that afternoon.

This was my first experience on an airplane. I didn't know anything, but I had heard of people getting air sick. I figured I would be one who got sick. When I boarded the plane, I grabbed my oxygen mask and put it on as high as it would go. I never got sick. I didn't realize I was the only one using the oxygen mask.

When we arrived over the London Airport, the pilot told us we could not land due to the dense fog covering the airport. He took us up above the fog. He was very calming in his tone and explanation of what was happening. When the fog lifted, we landed—in Ireland! The plane had to refuel. We were told we could get a bite to eat while the plane was refueling, but not to leave the airport.

Two English lady golfers had obviously noticed that I was an inexperienced flyer and took me in tow. "If they ask you if you want white, say yes," they advised. "But I don't use cream," I protested. "We know, but you will in this," they said as they nodded their heads and smiled at each other. We were served some sort of cooked cereal and meat, like streak-o-lean that was cooked so hard I had a tough time cutting it. The ladies helped me and when we had finished eating, we re-boarded the plane.

Jo stopped by the hospital to check on Mother before coming to the airport. To her surprise, the doctors said she could take Mother home. She was bruised and probably more than a little sore, but she would be fine.

When they arrived at the airport, they learned of the delay. They may have gotten something to eat to kill some time. Jo knew Mother was not a patient "waiter". By the time my plane landed, I picked up my luggage, and went through customs, she was definitely ready to go home—about another forty-five minute drive.

Jo was unable to have children, but she and Oscar adopted two boys. She had a lady nanny with the children. The older one attended an American school for the children of servicemen. The younger one was in day care. Oscar was at work and Jo was going to work. I went to bed. I think I slept the rest of the day. The nanny took care of Mother.

It was Market Day. Although there were several booths, there was only one item sold per booth. You had to go to different booths to get different items—nothing like the one-stop shopping markets in the USA. One of Jo's friends, a teacher, was interested in having me see and compare their facilities and curriculum with my own. She prepared a Tea at school to meet the parents. I thoroughly enjoyed it. Being a school teacher, I was always on the lookout for new and better ways to teach. In the Lunchroom just off the kitchen, was a mural of wheels the students had painted—huge wheels from ceiling to floor. It gave the optical illusion of being inside from one spot and on the outside from another spot. "I have to show this to everybody," the teacher said proudly. It was very impressive. There was a break room for students. When I stuck my head in, a boy sitting in the window sternly yelled at me, "This room is off limits to adults. Go to the teachers break room."

There was some kind of formal event on the base and Jo said I would need a hat or a veil. I didn't have either. We searched for a hat, but had to settle for a veil. None of the hats fit me. I spent most of my time with Mother. She was doing fine and I needed to go home. I was still working on my Specialist in Education Certificate. So on May 26th, I boarded my plane and returned home.

Shortly after getting back home, we took a trip to Jekyll Island with cousins Roland and Bessie. Then we toured East Kentucky with Hugh and Mildred Treadaway for about a week where we went by Natural Bridge—a huge rock formation which forms a "natural bridge"—and wound up in Boone County, Kentucky at Uncle Bruce and Aunt Florence's home. We usually visited them for a few days on each trip before we took I-75 and returned home.

On one visit, the church had planned a celebration honoring Aunt Florence as their Oldest Active Member. They really wanted it to be a surprise. Since we were regular visitors in their home, it did not raise any suspicion with Florence when we showed up. I believe she was totally surprised when John Bruce and his wife, one of the girls, who had sung with Billy's Band, Mary Elizabeth and her brother, Frank, Velma and her daughter, Ann, showed up at the church with Mulinix, the boys and me for the ceremony. Aunt Florence lived to be 92 years old and died May 28, 1996.

In July of 1967, Mulinix and I went to England on vacation. Jo met us at the airport, just as before. I saw her put something in Mulinix's hand and said, "This is for the Porter." We had money, but we were told later, not to spend American dollars, but to always get it exchanged into English pounds. It seems the Brits liked

American money and would hoard it—saving up for retirement, I guess. Anyhow, we always got our money exchanged before we went shopping.

On one shopping trip, I saw this beautiful unusual teapot. I asked, "How much?" The shopkeeper gave us a price "in American money". Jo shook her head, "No." Mulinix asked, "What is that in your money?" The shopkeeper acted as though he didn't understand and never would tell us an amount in the British pound. Mulinix would not let me buy the teapot. I was very disappointed, but I understood.

Years later, at a Flea Market, I saw a teapot almost identical to that one and I bought it for a lot less. I was very happy. I've always heard, "Good things come to those who wait."

We went to see a Shakespearean Play, the Changing of the Guard, Stratford, and where Wedgewood Pottery was made. We went to Lords of London, who had put out a little book honoring Americans who helped England during World War II. Mulinix's brother, Bill, was one who was killed in France. The book was kept at one of the Cathedrals. It was locked and once a day, the attendant would turn a page. If you wanted to see a name, he would open it and turn it with his white-gloved hand. It was in alphabetical order, supposedly, but we never found Bill's name. It was a huge disappointment, since it was one of the main reasons for going there.

While the nanny stayed with Mother and Jo's boys, we took a trip to Edinburg, Scotland. We all piled into the car. Oscar drove and Mulinix was the "co-pilot" or "navigator". However, when he got to the bottom of the page, he could not interpret the guide. Jo and Mulinix swapped seats. We made it to Edinburg where Jo had made reservations at a Bed and Breakfast.

We stayed three nights in Edinburg and toured the popular tourist attractions. We sent to the Castle, walked right in and saw the Queen's jewels, then on to another Cathedral. About two or three days later, we were back in London and went by another exhibition of the Queen's jewels. There was a line all the way around the building waiting to view the Jewels. Of course, there was much more than just the jewels. We decided it was unnecessary to wait in that long line. We went on and saw Big Ben, the London Bridge, and another Cathedral—St. Peter's, I think.

On our return from sightseeing, we visited the village of "Wall". It marked the place where the Roman Army's Northern Occupation was stopped when it invaded England. We were told the last of the Roman-built baths was there. We started out to see the baths, and instead of taking the path, like most other tourists, we cut across the pasture. The attendant had said, "It's just across the way." He failed to tell us that sheep also shared "the way" and Oscar stepped in "it". Some of the words that came out of his mouth were as offensive as what he had stepped in. We cleaned it off the best we could.

Along our route through the city of Mansfield, we found an Inn and were able to get adjacent rooms for the night. I was impressed by the size and the warmth of the bath towels. The Inn was also a gathering place for teenagers. It was so crowded that it was hard to get to the dining room. We ordered the strawberries and crème that the Inn was noted for. They were out. The waitress told us if we would come back early for breakfast, they would be serving them. But we had to be early, because they disappeared fast. We were early and got our strawberries and crème.

We went to a restaurant in Edinburg for dinner, where Oscar ordered a steak. The waitress came back to our table and said, "The steak is finished." I thought she meant the steak was from Finland—"Finnish". What she was actually saying, "We are out of steak. It's all gone."

The next weekend, Jo took us to London and checked us into another Bed and Breakfast. I thought it was peculiar when she took us by the train station. We were to ride the train back to Upper Heyford. Jo said, "This is where you will get off." Then she left us there and went back to Upper Heyford to work.

I was disappointed by one thing—I had envisioned a large, ornate railway station, like those in Atlanta. It was nothing but a locker room. You could put your stuff in a locker and return later to pick it up.

We finally learned how to get in a taxi, and get where we wanted to go by writing down the address, and using a map. They seemed to be able to understand our writing, but did not seem to understand our speech, nor we theirs, at times.

When we got on the train to return to Upper Heyford, we did not realize right away, that they were not calling out the upcoming stations. When I finally realized it and began to figure out where we were, I told Mulinix, "One more station." We got off at the right place. Unlike American train stations, the gate was on the train side, not the street side.

Mulinix and I went to a cafeteria to eat. We didn't recognize many of the food items. We slowly picked up a thing or two and the man behind us said, "You Americans. Get something and get out of the way." Very rude, I thought.

Julia Witherington wanted a postcard of the declining Shelley. The only place you could buy postcards of a particular place was at that particular place. All postcards were not sold at every location. We had to go out of our way a bit, but we finally got her postcard.

The time with Mother, Oscar and Jo's family was enjoyable and worth the trip. It was different. The people were definitely not "schooled in southern traditions or manners."

At the end of his three year assignment in England, they returned to the USA. Their household goods were to be delivered to a house he had received from his father's estate in Greensboro, GA. Sometime after the family got to Greensboro, their household goods were delivered. I was there when they were delivered and I sat on the porch marking off each item as it was delivered.

Each box was marked as to the placement of it in the house. If I didn't know where to put an item, I sent it to the rather large kitchen area. After some time and quite a few deliveries to the kitchen, I sent another piece to the kitchen and the Mover said, "Lady, have you seen that room? You can't put another piece in there."

When "Quitting Time" arrived, the movers started to leave. Oscar had just walked in. He asked, "What are you doing?" They said, "It's quittin' time. We're going home." "NO!" Oscar said as if commanding his troops. "You don't leave until every piece of furniture is in this house." Furniture was strewn all the way down the block. One of the pieces still on the lawn was Jo's Spinet Piano!

Later, Jo, Oscar, their boys, and Mother moved to Morrow, Georgia. That is where Mother died, after Cardiac Surgery, in 1982. She, too, is buried in the Annex to Oakland Cemetery in Rome, Georgia.

A Time to Say Farewell

I had taught and worked in the City School System six years. When my contract for the '67–'68 school year ended, I learned it had not been renewed. Mulinix and I discussed whether I should seek a teaching position elsewhere and we decided I would not. I quit teaching in the public school system.

For a time, I felt I was being hounded by the administration people, to make me feel guilty about quitting. However, the boys were almost through college. In fact, Gene had dropped out of college and enlisted in Officer Training in the Army. Unfortunately, after his second bout with pneumonia, he was told he would not be eligible, physically, to complete his Officer Training and was advised to get a medical discharge. He told them, "No", and asked what he would be eligible for. He finished his time in the regular ranks.

Victor only had one more year of College. He would graduate in 1969 and planned to teach after graduating. We had made our decision and we stuck to it.

Although I felt some sadness at the time, it turned out to be the best thing that could have happened to Mulinix and me. It had always been our dream to travel. For our immediate "future" we developed a new interest—camping!

Martha Frances and Rufus E Mulinix on their
wedding day December 23, 1943

Martha Frances and husband "Mulinix"
before he left for India 1944

Card designed and drawn by Martha Frances in high school to reflect her ambitions in life, Her Life Story.

Parents of Martha Frances, John Franklin
Hefner and Lula Puryear Hefner 1946

Back row, Mulinix, Martha, Velma, Mike,
Lula, Jo, Oscar w baby John
Front row Ann, Gene, Victor. Myra Lula's Family 1957 reunion

Photo that Mulinix carried in his wallet of Martha Frances until the day he died.

Mulinix, Martha Frances, Roland. Roland Puryear Martha's first cousin and the high school roommate of Mulinix 2009.

S. W. Puryear family at the 1933 family reunion in front of the store at Zone, Georgia. Martha Frances is on the front row holding the baby at the right end.

Anita Weinraub, LaVan Sturkey, Jane Barwick, Willene Free, Lucy Andree watching Flonnie Green put the last stitch in Mulinix's 90th birthday Quilt with Martha's assistance. 2012

Martha Frances, Mulinix, Victor and Gene
(Rufus Eugene Mulinix Jr.) 1958

Chapter Ten

CAMPING AND MUCH MORE

Between 1968, when I quit working in the school system, and 1983, when we took our first long trip, we made numerous short trips, craft shows, quilting classes, and demonstrations. During the summer of 1958, the boys had done some camping with the Boy Scouts. An interest in overnight camping became a growing thing. Our very first Mulinix family overnight campout was on the banks of the Etowah River on Spencer Fields property. Our nine-passenger station wagon was fitted with a mattress in the back for Mulinix and me. Behind the wagon were two folding cots with an old wool blanket rigged for a roof over the cots to protect the boys from the dew.

The boys couldn't wait to get in the water. As they felt their way through the water, Gene stepped on something that hurt his toe. He groped around and finally pulled up a 12" to 14" bayonet. They were close to the ford in the river and were told that soldiers in the Civil War used that ford to cross the river. The bayonet now resides in the Kingston Museum.

While camped at the river, we visited Spencer and he gave us some fresh corn. We took it back to camp and set it aside to prepare "in the morning". Much to our surprise, we were awakened in the night by two mules munching down on our corn.

When Mulinix and Roland came out of the service, they both came back to Georgia. Mulinix to the farm where he says he always knew was where he belonged with his Berry Sweetheart—"the best support system that any man can hope for."

Roland came back to the Atlanta area where he began working for Delta Airlines.

As Allatoona developed, several companies developed recreation areas for their employees. Delta was one of these and Roland and Bessie had a membership in Cushin Memorial Park on Allatoona, maintained under the auspices of Delta Airlines. It was a full service resort open to members and their guests only.

There was a swimming pool, boats for member's use, two areas marked off in the lake for swimming, and lots of skiing, swimming and eating. Roland's family shared their access to all the Lake activities with our family. We were guests there many times.

Roland and Bessie had two girls. Mulinix and I had two boys. Our boat would pull two skiers, but try as they might, they were never able to make it pull four. They did many things together through the years, and they had their differences.

However, none serious enough to break the relationships that developed.

Mulinix and I had a gate key and we would meet Roland and Bessie at the resort. Roland and Bessie would come from Riverdale and whoever got there first would begin to set up "camp". Mother went with us one time. She liked to eat fish. Bessie cooked some fresh fish and we all ate our fill. We came back to the cabin and Mother went straight to bed. When I got ready to go to bed, I heard Mother wheezing, gasping for breath, and barely calling my name. I went to check on her and she said, "I need help."

I replied, "Yessum, I guess we better get you some."

We had no idea where the hospital or a doctor was, but we started out and luckily found an all night gas station with an attendant who gave us directions to the hospital. We went to the emergency room and the attendant on duty began asking questions particularly about what we had eaten. When we mentioned fish, he came up with the diagnosis of a possible allergic reaction—to the fish probably. He said it almost certainly had been cooked in peanut oil. Mother was allergic to peanuts. He gave her a shot. In about 30 minutes she began breathing easier. We went back to the cabin and to bed.

In the morning, Mother was still in bed, and Mulinix and I were sipping on our coffee, when Roland came in. Roland had heard about the excitement of the night before. He was upset that we had not awakened them.

Mulinix asked, "Do you know where the hospital is?"

Roland replied, "No, but I would have found it."

Mulinix replied, "So did we—and you had uninterrupted sleep."

As time passed, our families grew and our schedules changed, and we drifted apart. Our concern for each other never diminished and showed when we were together.

Both Roland and Mulinix have brothers, but through their years of school and the service, they became closer than brothers. Roland would always tell Mulinix in parting, "Now you take care of our little girl." I was always "Little Girl" or "Sis".

Of the original four, three are gone.

While Mulinix was overseas, I had started a savings account in Millen. We always knew we wanted to travel. I transferred my savings account to a bank in Rome. Sometime later, Mulinix opened an account in Adairsville and we have banked there ever since. When the land next door to the our place came up for sale, Mulinix and his dad bought half a lot, about eighty acres. There went my savings. We wanted to buy a motor home, but to do that we had to sell some of the land, about one quarter of the lot.

E. G. Dickey had left the Education field and had become a Real Estate agent. He sold that part of the lot for us. In 1971, we bought a full blown motor home. We named it "Jonah" because something was always happening to it.

Soon after I quit teaching, I was invited to join a group called "The Art Council". The purpose of the group was to support and encourage the Arts in the local area. The following year the group decided to divide into teams by categories. One was in Crafts, another was Pottery, then Oils, and my special interest, Quilting.

Our Team held a meeting at 100 Mulinix Road. We were to do something and share it with the community. After much discussion, Mina Harper presented her idea—"I suggest we have a quilting class and Martha can teach it."

I shook my head and protested, "I can't teach it." Mina's rebuttal was, "Why not? You can quilt and you can teach."

Everyone seemed to be in agreement. I agreed with a stipulation that they would be my first class. I began to make some guidelines: My first quilting class was at 100 Mulinix Road in my living room. Each person chose their own project and we did our best to work through them. "The first classes could meet in my home; it would include this group only; each member would choose a project, keep lengthy notes on the procedures, and give constructive criticism. I had to feel my way as I went. It was a new experience for me as well—**teaching** quilting. Several had incomplete projects which we used to finish them up. Mina had a piece of patchwork she wanted to fix to go over the fireplace. The only one that actually got finished, I believe, was Mary Vaughn's "Patchwork Cushion".

We would evaluate the program in twelve weeks. If we were to continue, we would seek sponsorship from the Bartow Recreation Department."

I began to gather as much information as I could. I went to Stone Mountain once a week for six weeks and took a quilting class taught by Lorraine B. She worked in the gift shop and taught quilting classes in the evenings. I learned a lot of things from her.

The Rome Library was a part of the Inter-Learn System of the University System. They could get books on loan from any Library in that system. I checked out every quilt book I could find and requested some on loan. I bought books and brought them back to our class members, who could sign them out and use them at home. For a long time, we never lost or misplaced a book. Fortunately, when one was lost, it was one of mine. One day, almost a year later, the book was found under the sofa in one of the member's homes. We teased her about her house keeping for some time after that.

I made a work plan: Design and quilt two blocks—one on the quilting frame and one in their laps. I used colored sheets for the fabric. By the end of the course—five lessons—we had a show at Roselawn. Jimmy Davis got involved with Roselawn. It began to be used for receptions, weddings, and craft shows.

For a time we didn't have a regular meeting place. One year we had quilting classes in the field house at Cass High. One year we had a class at Beavers Senior Citizen Center. We had a quilt top in the quilting frame and one in a frame on display. We went to lunch and when we came back, the quilt in the frame was not mine. It was no where to be seen. Needless to say, we didn't go back. We finally settled on 100 Mulinix Road for our classes.

A couple of quilter's told us their husbands did most of the cooking because they quilted all the time. It has been said, "Quilters don't cook; quilters don't clean house; quilters QUILT!!"

Vic has been interested in reproductions of Early American furniture since he first began to show woodwork at craft shows. Each time he provided a display, he always included one copy of the Shaker Quilting Frame which his grandfather, Ben Mulinix, had made for his grandmother, Iva L. Fields Mulinix. The only person we knew who remembered quilting on her mother's frame was Sara Lou, Mulinix's sister. She helped us figure out what was needed to make the frame work. When we tried to use the frame we ran into problems, but we kept trying until we got it working. Our first presentation of frames was at a Needlework show in Rome. Word had gotten around that Victor had copied Grandmother's Freestanding Quilting Frame. Margaret Gaylor, Home Extension Agent for Floyd County, invited Victor to show and demonstrate the frame. He had the frame but no quilt top. We borrowed a "Double Wedding Ring" quilt top from Sara Lou, Mulinix's sister. The frame was a very popular spot in the show. People began asking him about making the frames for sale. He agreed and we started making a list of orders.

After the show, Victor finished one frame right away. The others were being pushed back for other "interests". He was teaching in Jacksonville, Florida at the time and visits home were to see Marty, not woodwork. Everywhere we went, people asked about their frames. Mulinix got tired of explaining and began making the frames himself. He did this for years, even before retiring from General Electric. Mulinix and I delivered, set up and demonstrated the use of the frames by putting a quilt top in the frame.

One day a couple came to our house to pick up their frames. As I was showing the wife how to put the materials in the frame, the husband sat in a chair looking around the room. He asked, "How many of the things in this room are for sale?" A little surprised, I replied, "None!"

He said, "I've been in antique stores that didn't have as much in them as you have in this room."

We finished the demonstration and began to take the quilt and frame down. We would have delivered it, but the wife said she believed she could do it, so we loaded the frame and they took it home.

In the summer of 1970, in the cab-over camper, we went to the Outer banks of North Carolina where we climbed all the way to the top of a lighthouse. We went through a coal mining area in West Virginia where there was construction all the way through the mountains. In Arkansas, I bought "diamond" (crystal) brooches for high-neck dresses and Christmas gifts for the girls.

Right after we purchased Jonah in 1971, Mulinix and I went by way of Alabama to the Natchez Trace. We hit it about midway and went to the south end and retraced our way back to the north end, stopping at all marked points of interest. It seemed every time we got out of the motor home and back in, there was a tick on me. We tracked ticks all the way up the Natchez Trace.

As the equipment changed, our companions changed. We became interested in outdoor dramas such as: "The Lost Colony"—the story of a group of settlers who disappeared. A search expedition was sent, but the settlers were never found.

The Indian drama "Unto These Hills" at Cherokee, North Carolina—was more than a one-time trip for the family. We went to a musical drama in Kentucky and in Hannibal, Missouri a Mark Twain Drama.

We toured East Kentucky with Hugh and Mildred Treadaway for about a week where we went by Natural Bridge—a huge rock formation which forms a "natural bridge"—and wound up in Boone County, Kentucky at Uncle Bruce and Aunt Florence's home for a few days before we returned home.

The first big craft show we attended was in 1973 at Powers Crossroads County Fair and Arts Festival, near Newnan, Georgia. I had seen an advertisement about it and suggested it might be something Victor should check into. Mulinix and I would go along and be chief cooks and bottle washers.

As it turned out, Mulinix and Victor made wooden toys. I took along some Job's Tears and Indian Corn Beads. When we arrived, we realized they were interested in demonstration as much or more than displays. I began to string Job's Tears making bracelets, necklaces, etc. I had a basket of Indian Corn semi shucked on display. Corn Beads were a novelty.

One little girl had been watching me. Victor had been watching her. She had a nickel she wanted to use to buy something. She had been talking to Victor and he told her to come to me and see what I could do for her. She came up to me and said, "He said you could make something for me." So I measured her finger and put a bead of Job's Tears on a string and tied it on her index finger. She went around holding up her finger ring for everyone to see. A lady with her, possibly her grandmother, said, "Thank you. Thank you. Thank you. We didn't know what we were going to do with that nickel." I tried to give the nickel back, but she wouldn't take it. She rejoined the child.

We had a good time, but did very little cooking. Victor made several items on the spot. Marty displayed some of her crocheted items and assisted everywhere she was needed. Mulinix wrote the receipts because we had to account for our money. We continued doing this craft show for many years.

The weekend after Labor Day weekend, we did a repeat performance at the Pine Log Arts and Crafts Show at the Pine Log Campground. We used the porch of one of the houses for our display and stayed in our Motor Home. We learned to bring our own food because buying the food there ate up any profit we might make. This also became a yearly show.

Bartow County Recreation Department sponsored a quilt and crafts show at Roselawn. This was an ongoing thing for several years. I had been asked to instruct participants in the quilting area. We displayed some of our quilts and had a quilt in the frame for demonstrating the procedure of quilting. Viewers could even add a few stitches for on-hands learning.

There were many other shows in which we participated year after year: Crowe Springs Craftsmen Fair in Cartersville, usually in October; Chiaha Harvest Fair the following week in October, in Rome; Stilesboro Academy—Chrysanthemum Show; The Berry Patch at Berry High School—only one time; "Quilt-In" at Bartow County Library in February of 1985 and 1986; Quilting at the Tullie Smith House at the Atlanta Historical Society from 1985-1/1993; "Quilting with Mulinix" at Stone Mountain Park's "Old South Celebration, July 30, 1985; and we did "Show and Sell" for two days in Kingston. The Woman's History Club sponsored it and it did real well the first year. However, the second year, we did not do anything. It rained.

We did volunteer work for the Department of Tourism. We went to Atlanta and did demonstrations of quilting frames and quilting.

We went to Beaver Creek in Rockmart, GA. to deliver a set of frames to a lady teaching three quilting classes—one in the morning, one in the afternoon, and one at night. We did a demonstration of the frame and came home with orders for 15-20 frames.

We met a lady who was trying to make a quilt for a wedding in a very short time. She bought one of our frames and, as usual, we helped get it set up with a quilt top in the frame. I realized she was not going to have enough time to quilt the traditional way, so I taught her another way, tacking. She had some "Cheater Cloth", pre printed designs. Since the inside of the material was not separated it did not need close quilting. Quilting is like making a sandwich, the top, the batting, then the lining or backing. She bought her materials on Monday, Mulinix and I helped her. We went back on Friday and helped her finish the quilt. She was able to finish the quilt in time for the wedding.

One thing you could not help noticing when you entered her house—it was totally lined in plastic! The furniture, the walls, the floors—everything was protected in plastic. I had never seen anything like it before or since. She was taking care of her elderly mother and maybe that had something to do with the plastic. I don't know.

Mulinix never charged more than $150-$175 for both the large and the small frames. We had one lady who had bought two sets of quilting frames from us. She was in the service and was being sent overseas. In packing their belongings, each item had to be appraised and a value assigned for insurance purposes. One set of quilting frames was appraised at $400. She had two, so it was $800.

One of our neighbors had gotten a set of frames from someone who owed him money. He went to collect his money and the person could not pay. He saw the quilting frame hanging on the porch and said he would take the frame in payment for the money owed to him. The other person wasn't too excited about it, but he didn't have the money. The neighbor still has the frames.

I have continued to be very much involved with quilting and quilting activities. Working with other volunteers we made an inventory of quilts in Georgia, which resulted in the publication of Georgia Quilts. I was responsible for one chapter entitled "Cover: Everyday Quilts". We documented quilts under the editorship of Anita Weinraub and with quilting groups throughout Georgia.

Chapter Eleven

KINGSTON MUSEUM

1949 through the present

Museums became one of the main points of interest wherever we went. As we spent more and more time on the road, we visited many small museums. Always noticing how things were done and talking with, in most cases, amateur historians about ways and means to preserve local history.

That's what the Kingston Woman's History Club does—preserving local history and presenting it to the public.

When I first joined the Kingston Woman's History Club, I learned one of the projects they were interested in was a museum—to preserve the memories of yesterday and the dreams of tomorrow. KWHC had been working to have a museum in our community for some time. We visited a hotel in Marietta with a museum. We visited the Atlanta History Museum, always asking questions and taking notes on how to display items in a museum. Still, the beginnings were very slow.

As early as 1949, Museum Committee Members, Margie Roberts, Betty Joyce Jolly, and I put together a small one-room museum in the Kingston Hotel just off the main lobby. The hotel was owned by Margie Roberts.

Through a long standing acquaintance of Margie's, Col. B. C. Yates, Director of Kennesaw Mountain Battlefield State Park, we acquired four large panels which depicted the most active involvement of Kingston in the War. The first panel depicted "The Cotton Kingdom and the Affluent Plantations". The second and third panels depicted "Incidents of Kingston's Involvement in the War". The fourth panel depicted "The Confederate Memorial Day Observances". They were first displayed at the Memorial Service at Kingston Baptist Church. Then they were moved to the Kingston Hotel.

In 1960, the interest in a museum began to grow when Representatives Henry A. Keever and Woodrow Bradley secured an acre of land for the City of Kingston for the purpose of erecting a Confederate Memorial Museum. One stipulation was, to have plans for, or to have a building on site in ten years.

I believe it was in Ola Mac Andrew's first term as President of KWHC that she appointed an actual Museum Building Committee. The members of the committee included Ola Mac Andrews, Betty Joyce Jolly, Margie Roberts, and me.

We began to make appeals to everybody we knew for anything we needed or for donations of anything pertaining to Kingston's History. We had many fundraisers. There were chicken suppers with slide shows of local scenes taken by Mulinix and the boys. The movie house began showing a black and white film made in 1946 about Kingston. We were able to make copies and sell them.

Mrs. Lois Malone had a kinsman who was experimenting with some new designs for concrete blocks—and yes—our first building was made from those blocks.

Ayler Gallagher used to call it the "Hen House" because only women ever went there. Some time between obtaining the land and the actual construction of the museum, Margie Roberts sold the hotel. The members were very creative in finding a place for all items. The panels were moved to Ayler Gallagher's shop/office building. Most of the smaller stuff like mini balls to cannon balls, shards of Indian Pottery to polished gravel, found a resting place under the beds of various KWHC members.

This situation brought more attention to the need for a building to store all the artifacts. In 1970, the Plans were finalized and construction on the building began. In 1971, the Kingston Confederate Memorial Museum was presented to the public. There was much more interest and we had a lot of people who did a lot of things for us. Donations kept coming in. As time passed and more people made donations, the Museum was packed to overflow. Talk began about an Annex.

One donation which came by way of Mr. Watson B. Dyer, was a big antique chest of drawers which had been at the Georgia Capitol during the second term of Governor Brown. We called it "Governor Brown's Drawers".

Mr. Dyer was very interested in the museum, which was now bulging at the seams. He asked me "When are you going to get an Annex built?" I told him, "We have no funds except for the prize egg left over from an Easter Egg Hunt—we need more than $1.00.

"Well, let's get that fund started today," he said, and he handed me a check for $500.00. Our balance jumped to $501.00. Another drive began for funds or donations of memorabilia pertaining to Kingston's history.

In 1997, a Ground Breaking Ceremony was held on August 15, for what would become the Martha Mulinix Museum Annex. Our Mayor at the time, Margo Martin, supervised much of the construction and helped acquire some of the materials.

Many people worked on the building and we furnished lunch for them. There was one man in particular who furnished the idea for the banisters on the back stoop. He worked diligently. They looked nicer, but took longer to make. He said, "All I have to give is my time." We received no funds from our County Commissioner, Clarence Brown. There was some technicality. However, he was able to help in other ways.

Georgia Power Economist, Rachel Cantrell, wanted to donate the kitchen. However, some appliances had already been donated. She agreed to let the amount that had been designated for this project remain the same. We were in bad need of a lighting system. I believe it was approved by a top official of Georgia Power in Rome, to use the balance of those funds for this purpose.

Much of the remaining work was done on a pay as you go basis. As money came in, another project was completed. By 1998, "The Martha Mulinix Museum Annex" was completed and dedicated.

From the beginning, the City of Kingston paid the utilities until the economy began to slow down and money got tight. Out of necessity, they withdrew that support and the museum began to pay those items. This meant more fundraisers and membership dues. Hopefully, the City will be able to provide that support again soon.

Over the years, we lost Mrs. Ola Mac Andrews, Mrs. Bessie Gallagher, and Mrs. Betty Joyce Jolly in death. Margie Roberts had sold the hotel and moved away. My health and that of Mulinix began to limit our involvement. Others stepped up to fill the vacancies.

In spite of their many efforts, interest in the museum and Kingston's role in history seems to have waned to some extent. There is so much history about Kingston that many of the residents may not know. It is well worth a visit to educate our children on the role Kingston people have played in history.

Phyllis Casey and Marty Mulinix have worked hard to get everything into the computer. They're working toward having a dual list—one in the museum, and one elsewhere.

Ayler Gallagher used to say, "Martha got fired. I retired, and we built a museum!"

"We"—the people—built the museum. Ayler and I were privileged to be a part of it.

Chapter Twelve

THE KNOXVILLE WORLD'S FAIR

September, 1982

Gene and Judy Mulinix went to the Knoxville World's Fair. When they returned, they were telling us about the fair, and Judy said the quilts in the exhibit were not as good as what she had seen of my quilts. She thought I should apply to become a participant in the Fair.

I obtained an application, filled it out, and put it in the mail along with a letter giving some background on my knowledge of and my connection to Appalachia.

Within a day or two, I received a phone call from the World's Fair Official asking me if I could come "today". I told him, "No, I can't come today! I have to wash, pack, refurbish my motor home—I have to prepare."

"We'll furnish you a place to stay and meals," he replied.

I would need a quilt top to demonstrate and for a display. I went to Eva Young. Using the "Around the Mountain" pattern, Eva pieced a top of prints adding a wide, solid, blue border. She left a place in the corners for the World's Fair Flame Emblem. The colors were red, white, and blue. There were four of us. Each one took a corner. We put the flame emblem on the quilt, on my skirt, and on a jacket.

When the preparations were completed, we headed to Knoxville. On arrival in Knoxville, we were assigned to one of the renovated apartments housing the Fair participants. There were about five other participants in other apartments.

Breakfast was ready when we got up the next morning. There was a vehicle waiting to take us to the Fairgrounds to set up. They had someone watching and available to answer any question we might have. After about the third day, I guess they decided we knew what we were doing, and their requirements were being met, and they left us alone.

A young man who was in the service, came by our booth and said, "I have always wanted to learn to quilt."

"Really," I asked. "Well, let's see what we can do about that."

I got him started and taught him how to hide the knot. He stayed with us all day. I checked on him frequently, as he continued to quilt. By the end of the day, he said he felt like he could quilt now and I agreed. He helped us close up. We never heard from him again.

We took the sky lift that overlooked the exhibits. It was free for us. I thought the view of the fairground and the exhibits was impressive. I enjoyed it very much. Mulinix, however, did not care much for it.

When our allotted time for display and demonstration was over, we received an invitation to participate in, what they called "Best of Show". Those who were in this group were chosen by the Fair Officials. This is where we met the "Masters of Their Trade" from each category.

Leaving the Fairground, we went to North Kentucky to visit Aunt Florence until the "Best of Show" exhibit at the end of the Fair. She had invited some friends in who had never done any quilting. We worked on a variation of "Around the Mountain" with the colors being gold, brown and green. We had the most fun.

Time flies when you're having fun, and soon we had to go back to the Fairground to set up our display again. This time we were housed in a motel overlooking the Fairground. Our fellow exhibitors were, for the most part, well-known "Masters of Their Trade".

One lady came up to me and asked how much I had to pay to use "the emblem". I told her I paid nothing. She said she was told she could not use the emblem without paying a $500.00 fee. No one ever approached me or said anything to me. I guess it's true sometimes, "Ignorance is bliss," also cheap.

After we got our exhibit set up, we had a little free time. We made one last trip to the gift shop. I bought a few little knick knacks to give to the kids and to a few others who had helped us. We went back to our room to pack and wait for the closing fireworks. We had an excellent view from our balcony. It was a good experience and one we would remember with a smile.

Back home, things were beginning to wind down for the holidays. Just a few more quilt shows, Thanksgiving Dinner and our Christmas Eve Family dinner. The year would be ending soon.

Plans for our first long trip were coming together and we were getting excited. Still there were things to do on the farm before we could turn loose. Gardens had to be prepared and planted. Vineyards needed to be pruned. Supplies for the trip needed to be gathered and packed. Really, not too much time if you think about it.

Time passed quickly. The day of our departure had arrived—May 6, 1983.

Chapter Thirteen

AS FAR WEST AS THE GRAND CANYON

Jonah's Journey #1
May 6-June 17, 1983
Including Overnight Trip to Mexico with Roger and Fred
4,772.5 Miles 6 Weeks

Jonah was packed with everything from food and linens to maps and spare auto parts. We were on our way—destination—the Grand Canyon. We filled up at KOA in Cassville, GA. We had only gone 135 miles when we had to make a stop in Anniston, Alabama. We had to have the electronic ignition removed and the points replaced at Crowe and Patterson Auto Repair Shop. We camped for the night at Riverside, Alabama beside the Coosa River. There, I added 1 brown Root Beer bottle, 1 Coke bottle, and 1 piece of driftwood to my growing collection of memorabilia. Mulinix learned early on if he helped me find memorabilia such as this, I spent a lot less time in gift and souvenir shops.

We generally traveled from state park to state park because they usually had what their brochure advertised, and they were well maintained. As soon as we were situated in our "home base", we looked for a church and a Laundromat. Most of the churches were Baptist, although not many were Southern Baptist.

On May 10, we installed a new "John" in Jonah. Then we went to Louisiana to visit friends, Ben and Dot Doss, who graduated with us from high school. We had a delicious seafood dinner. While in Louisiana, we visited Avery Island where the Tabasco Pepper Sauce Factory is located, then the Jungle Gardens and Bird City—a pier-like structure that egrets use for nesting. We visited the Longfellow-Evangeline Area, where the grave site of Evangeline is located in the Catholic Cemetery. We got permission from Mr. Powell, the caretaker, to stay in the parking lot until the Acadian Village opened. We had a very nice visit with Mr. Powell and his daughter. They introduced us to "slave cotton"—a brownish cotton not market worthy, but slaves could buy and sell it.

At St. Martinville, Louisiana, we stumbled into an active quilting group who welcomed us to join in their quilting activity. When the Acadian Village opened, we went with a second grade class—one of many grades taking the tour. We left there and checked in at the Sam Houston State Park in Lake Charles, Louisiana. I found a duck egg. I carried it around for two or three years. A lady in our quilting group was going to make something for me with the egg, but she quit coming to our group and I threw the egg away.

We went through Beaumont, Texas and Gladys City Boom Town—Oil Gusher in early 1900s.—an outdoor Living History Museum operated by Lamar University. We went on to San Felipe, Texas and stopped at Stephen Foster State Park for a day of rest. I used my machine and did some sewing on my patchwork. Mulinix had to borrow a ladder from our neighbor, Mr. Massey, to un-clog the drain on the air conditioner.

Back on the road, we stopped at Sealy, Texas to do some laundry then on to Palmetto State Park near Gonzales, Texas. We enjoyed Gonzales—especially the displays at the "Old Jail" Museum with a former Georgian as the attendant.

At Lockhart State Recreation Area we made our weekly phone call and finished the patchwork sampler of the August Show Quilt. It hangs in my kitchen. It was to be used in the August Show at the Gallery in Cartersville. We photographed it against the Grand Canyon background.

We were on the road again, to San Antonio, Texas and a week with Roger Gallagher and Fred. The first night there, we were in Jonah when a terrible rain storm came up. The winds were so strong it had blown water under the door in Roger's house. He came out and insisted we stay in his spare room because the weather reports were calling for flash floods, heavy thunderstorms, and a possible tornado watch in the Houston area. I think he was afraid Jonah would blow over. We stayed there most of the week.

Each day, Roger had something planned for us to do or see. One morning he came in and said, "San Antonio has at least three large museums—"The Alamo", "The Southwest Craft Center", and "The Texas Longhorn Hall of History". Which one do you want to visit?"

To which I replied, "Why can't we visit all three?"

With a surprised look on his face he said, "Well, it might be a lot of walking, but I guess we can do that—if you're up to it." We ate at the "Copper Kitchen" then Mulinix found and bought a belt buckle souvenir.

After the museums, Fred insisted we just had to take a trip to Mexico. We went to church at the First Baptist Church of Helotes where the Purple Sage was in full bloom. It seems it blooms after a rain. We attended a "Free Dance" family night at the Helotes General Store.

Motel Casablanca . . . . SHOPS!!! The government shops had the largest offering and the best prices. I did some Christmas shopping. I found some small, cup-size, black clay bells, and some larger tea glass size, green, clay bells that were about 7 cents each. I bought 25 or 30 to be used on the table at our Christmas Eve Dinner.

The prices were so much less than at home. I was on a shopping frenzy—baskets, bells, bottles, and bags. It was getting late. Dinner was every man for himself—tough on the waiter. We spent the night.

In the morning Fred took us sightseeing. We went to a fabric shop where I tried to buy some fabric. Fred said, "Tell Me, Martha." So I told him, "I want some fabric like a Mexican woman would buy." Needless to say, I got it, but not without Fred's help.

About lunchtime, we left Mexico and went to Eagle Pass, Texas for lunch at a restaurant Fred recommended. He was very careful about the foods we ate. We did not drink the water while in Mexico. IT'S GREAT TO BE AN AMERICAN!!!

After we had eaten, we returned to San Antonio for one more night with Roger and Fred. When morning came, we told our hosts "goodbye"—knowing we would not receive such royal treatment anywhere else.

On to Kerrville State Park in Kerrville, Texas and the Kerrville Craft Show on May 27th. There were large tent poles down the middle of the road, with displays on the sides—maybe as long as a football field. I watched for something to bring back to Gene and

Victor. There was a young girl who had a tortilla warmer for sale. I bought three of them. Later, we were just about to leave, when this same girl came up to me, very excited, and thanked me for buying the tortilla warmers. She explained that she had not sold anything during the whole show until I bought the tortilla warmers. After that, the people watching wanted to know if there were any more. They began buying everything she had. She had nearly sold out.

Jonah must have been feeling neglected. He was "drooping". The right front tire was 10 lbs low. We changed to the spare tire and found a Firestone store and had the tire repaired. We also located a Supermarket and bought groceries.

We had to change campgrounds because State Park could only take us for Thursday night. We had made reservations for the weekend at Ranchero Vista. The ad for the Park said "Laundry"—we washed! I finished the edges of the August Sampler Quilt. This park was having a difficult time staying open—they were exceptionally friendly and helpful. We toured the Caverns of Sonora—a study of sculpture in color. We checked into the camp at Ozona Inn and had dinner at the Inn. There was a rainstorm and we had water problems to make the night memorable.

On May 31st, Mulinix walked to town to try to get parts for the water system. After the repairs, we checked in at the Davis Mountain State Park near Fort Davis and visited Fort Davis. We hiked up the mountain far enough to see the whole camp and lodge. We could also see the mist begin to roll in. We backtracked to the Park for gas. One of the largest telescopes in the world is located here.

We followed TX118 for 52 miles through lonely, but breathtaking mountains and arrived in Kent. We found the El Paso Information Center and the Museum of History. We bought a beautiful Indian Design Scarf then checked in at the Roadrunner RV Park.

June 2nd—We washed clothes and hair. We went to the Tigna Indian Reservation where we bought some Indian Bread—similar to sour dough—in large round loaf. We used it for cheese and meat sandwiches for lunch. We drove to Arial Tramway and rode to the top of Ranger Peak. It was a frightening hairpin-turn road to the Tramway and very steep. Jonah got hot!! Mulinix did more maintenance work—added antifreeze. More walking—more sand.

We left the Roadrunner RV Park and El Paso and went to the North Mexico Welcome Center—NOT OPEN! In Deming, NM we bought gas entirely in liters and it was priced per liter—.30 1/10. It took 142 6/10 liters. (How's your math?)

We had lunch at City of Rocks State Park and crossed the Continental Divide northwest of Silver City, New Mexico. At the Gila National Forest, we made our first stop for a "vapor lock", then the air conditioner went "bump".

We had to repair Jonah's water system, and in Flagstaff, two days later, Jonah just balked. We stumbled into a camp—Mayse Canal Travel Trailer Park where we slept under sleeping bags. B-R-R-R!

June 4th—Alpine—Alps of Arizona—We had a slow start. At the first gas stop, water froze when the attendant tried to clean the windshield. The temperature was 27-28 degrees! The next stop was at Petrified Forest National Park. We stopped for wood before entering the Park. We walked in "Rainbow Forest", ate lunch at the Santa Fe RR Exhibit, and drove to Northern Flagstaff, Arizona Gas Service Center. We had been assured that they would install the air conditioner!!

Mulinix walked across the highway and registered at the KOA. We had dinner at a nearby Inn before entering the campground. We walked behind the camp at the base of the mountain. Yellow Pine **IS** yellow—even dead fallen trees!

We spent a full day at the KOA. The resident mechanic had to install parts from our reserve of "spares".

We learn something every day! On the camp "nature walk" we learned that those tall yellow barked pines we called "Yellow Pines" yesterday, are really Ponderosas!

The Shopping Center and Mall across the highway proved to be a source for film processing, which we had been hunting for several days.

We left Flagstaff and went to the Grand Canyon Camper Village in Tusayan, AZ. We registered then took a shuttle bus to the Canyon. We got our first view of the Canyon at Mather Point then toured the West Rim via the National Park Shuttle. There were Indian Dancers at the Campground "after dark"—8:00 Indian Time.

June 7th, we walked to the Helicopter Terminal. The flight over the Canyon was very interesting! We had considered taking the mule train ride through the Canyon, but decided against it. When we got there, we learned there was a weight limit on that tour. Mulinix would not have been able to go. The pilot was concerned about me losing my hat until I showed him how many bobby pins I had holding it on. He finally determined it would be safe.

During the tour from the sky, I couldn't help noticing the similarities of colors in the Canyon and those in the mini-quilt I had just finished. It was a duplicate of one on loan to the Bartow County History Museum. Later, we came back and took pictures with the Canyon as the background for comparison.

We went into all the nearby shops. The area reminded us of the Smokies! Nice crafts BUT also "junque" galore! Today, we mainly looked then drove to the Park, parked Jonah at Yavapai Point and went by shuttle to Bright Angel Lodge. We looked around while waiting for the Fred Harvey East Rim Tour to begin. Fran, our driver-guide, was excellent. We learned much about the Canyon. We photographed the August Sampler at the Canyon Rim. The colors of the Canyon and those in the Miniature quilt are the same. These are also the colors of the Art Council Gallery in Cartersville, GA. We planned to display this miniature quilt in the next showing at the Gallery.

Fred Harvey is the Commissioner at the park. Babbitt is a name seen everywhere. He has General Stores at several locations. The campground owner is also, Governor of Arizona. We left the Grand Canyon Camper Village and ate lunch at Walnut Canyon near Flagstaff. We walked the trail through cliff dwellings. We used our Golden Age Passport at Walnut Canyon. We stopped at Geronimo's Indian place, and checked in at Holbrook, AZ KOA by mid-afternoon. We did some laundry then watched a Mexican folk dance program. Before leaving AZ, I made my "Indian stop" at Cree's Indian Store on the Navajo Reservation. Arelia Bejay posed with her rug in progress for us.

We ate lunch at a roadside park in the Malpain Lava Flow area—made some pictures—walked or climbed the rocks, then went through Albuquerque, NM—one lane because of paving in progress.

We bought groceries, did one load of laundry, washed hair and Mulinix found a barber.

On June 11, we got up early and Mulinix said, "Let's go home."

I looked at him and said, "What!"

He looked at me and again said, "We need to go home."

So, at 6:55 am, we started home, which made the need for the air conditioner unnecessary until about lunch time. When we turned it on, it wouldn't work! We began searching the Guide for a mechanic. The first call, we received no answer. On a Saturday afternoon, we considered ourselves very fortunate to find a mechanic who would even look at the AC . . . His solution—he removed the **overlooked packing** from the fan—charged $10.00.

When we traveled, Mulinix liked to sleep late. Working third shift, he would come home at 11:30 p.m. We would have some dessert—cake and coffee—then we would go to bed. I took a big basket full of maps, information sheets, and books on the sites we were going to see. I would read and when he woke up, we would discuss which sites and routes we were going to take.

We left Amarillo and stopped at a small roadside park called "Circle C". We walked a "sand" road and found gourds almost mature. We had Sand Spurs on our clothes when we returned. Roger Gallagher says in Texas, they are called "Stikker Burrs."

Sunday, we attended church in Clarendon, Texas at the Calvary Baptist Church. Afterward we went to a roadside picnic area for lunch then to Wichita Falls to Lake Arrowhead State Recreation Area. A working oil well just in front of our camp had the label "Walsh and Watt, Inc. Morris "B" Lease Well # 3".

Our last Texas "do"—Marshall Pottery. It reminded me of Wedgwood "Production Craftsman" assembly line. We followed the guide to Monroe, LA KOA. It turned out to be our Kampground.

In Cuba, AL at the "Old McGowan Place", we met Linda and Charlie Munoz. They carried us to their home, an antebellum that they are "loving back to life". The doors that quilting can open! We paused at Bluff Hall in Demopolis.

Traveling on, we came to Mound State Monument, Moundville, AL. We called Victor. He told us he would cook supper! We slipped in and out of clouds all day. At lunch time, in Anniston, AL we went to K-Mart to buy cubes for slides. We ate lunch at Morrison's. A sudden downpour made a bookstore stop necessary. We found a book, "Advanced Quilting".

At 1:35 pm Alabama time, 2:35 pm Georgia time, we crossed the state line. We stopped at Cowan Hardware and made phone calls. Gene had called and said Maurice Hohn had died. I finally got through to Doris Hohn and told her we would go home and get some clean linens, unload and put Jonah in her back yard for a "spare bedroom".

We pulled out all our mementoes—just what everybody needs—more stuff with no place to stuff it!

By the end of the day, we were in Victor's yard in Lithia Springs. The next morning, June 17th, we left Lithia Springs at 7:35 am, made a stop at the Kroger in Cartersville and by 10:08 am, we were HOME. Jonah's Journey #1 had come to an end. The miles traveled by Jonah—4,772.5.

Chapter Fourteen

AS FAR NORTH AS THE SOURCE OF THE MISSISSIPPI

Jonah's Journey #2
May 10 – July 7 1984
5,011.6 Miles 9 weeks

Jonah's Journey '84 – Through the years we have been privileged to have some interesting travel experiences and we still have a long list of places we would like to see. But Jonah's Journey for '84, which started May 10, 1984 carried us to one place that has been high on our list of priorities for many years – Lake Itasca, Minnesota, the source or headwaters of the Great Mississippi River.

On day 1 of our journey, we went as far as Gadsden, Alabama and spent the night at Noccalula Falls Park. Our very first view of the falls included a rainbow! There was a statue beside the falls which just set the stage for the lore and legends we learned there.

Gilliland Covered Bridge forms the entry into the Pioneer Homestead part of the park. There was a very interesting collection of homes and out-buildings representing life in earlier days. There was a log cabin with many quilts spread around inside – one very pleasing patchwork for which I do not know the name.

The Noccalula Falls stop saw the beginning of the routine which we began to follow – a limited amount of mileage covered each day, some time spent walking and exploring our surroundings and locating a laundryomat and a church.

In Huntsville, we found RV parking within walking distance of the Space Center and we settled in. Then we "made like tourists" and took a bus tour through the facilities. We made three stops on the tour bus: The Sky Lab; The Neutral Buoyancy Simulator; and The Shuttle Orbits Mock-up. We had lunch on the "Lunch Pad" which provided an over-all view of the outside exhibit area of the Space Museum. Mulinix found a blue hat.

From the "experiences" for the young folk [the rules kept us out], to the exhibits showing actual equipment, to the movies in the Space Dome, we felt that the presentations were very commendable.

Navigation Locks along the Tennessee River furnished our first contact with the River transportation for which we never lost our fascination. At Wheeler Dam we walked on the locks. We learned that the "lift" for Wheeler is 47 feet. At Wilson the locks "lift" 100 feet – the tallest such "lift" in the world.

Water does run downhill and although it might skip along by waterfalls and shoals, in order for boats and barges to navigate, there must be some way other than "running the rapids". Therefore: Navigation Locks. We did become a little more knowledgeable about them as our journey progressed.

In Florence, Alabama an Indian Mound, which we had looked forward to seeing, was closed because of floodwaters. This was the first of a long line of frustrations and plan modifications that would result from the seasonal high waters throughout the trip.

Our first view of McPharland Park seemed to indicate that the water was "up". And sure enough, there was no way we could get to the camping area. But a ranger was stationed at the roadblock to direct us to alternate facilities.

The next morning we visited Pope's Tavern, Florence's oldest structure. It was built as a Stage Stop and Tavern in 1811 and became a museum in 1960. It had a folding bed which came from a New England Tavern, we were told. There were other antique beds and none of them looked very comfortable. They were covered with some beautiful quilts. One had a feathered wreath in the open squares. There was even a cradle with a bit of patchwork in it.

Roadside signs for "Connor's Pottery" (near Ashland, Mississippi) drew us off the road for a lunch stop. There was a round brick structure which was an early kiln – telling us that once pottery was probably made here. But the wares we saw displayed were not pottery but cast statuary much like we are familiar with and have the concrete coatings which are not kiln dried.

In the outskirts of Memphis, Tennessee, at T. O. Fuller State Park, we entered the Indian Interpretative Area through an actual mound.

We viewed restorations as well as Indian remains and artifacts like a fish basket on a shelf.

Wood Bell is a working craftsman at Chucalissa, which is Choctaw for "abandoned houses". He grew up on a Choctaw Reservation in Central Mississippi. His sister, Minnie, made split cane baskets. When I asked if he helped her in any way, he shook his head "no, no…somebody else do it."

Mud Island is a tourist attraction in downtown Memphis that lives up to its highest billing. We entered by way of the Monorail. The complex contains a scale model of the Mississippi River running the length of the island. You can see the twists and turns of the great river as it makes its way to the Sea. You can see where the bridges are located and figure out the sizes of the towns along the way. I was disappointed to find the northern section of the watershed depicted by a fountain, but as a whole, Mud Island is outstanding. In the museum we saw a movie featuring John Chappell as Mark Twain, interpreting the park and since we had earlier had opportunity to hear Chappell in person portraying Mark Twain, we found this especially meaningful.

Mud Island has a variety of shops. In one called "River Crafts" we found some familiar quilts – Flower Garden, Log Cabin, Colonial Doll – but for us at least, unfamiliar prices. (The cheapest was $325.00.)

Next stop Memphis, Tennessee for our first Cruise on "Ole Man River" aboard the Memphis Queen III. We began to see some Mississippi floodwaters. We were told that the river was at the highest it had been since 1973. I found going under the bridges a bit frightening.

We were aware that there is a Mississippi Parkway Commission and Great River Road Association, but we did not secure their guide until we reached Memphis. However, for the remainder of our time along the river we learned to rely on the information this handy little guide provided. We took a side trip suggested by the guide to the Civil War Fort Pillow. Here you could see how the course of the Mississippi is constantly changing with a comparison of the river during the Civil War time and the present location of the river. However, the breastworks built in 1861 are at their usual location. Incidentally, General Nathan Bedford Forrest, (Forrest Hotel, Rome) saw action at Fort Pillow. The young ranger on duty at Fort Pillow didn't seem to have much knowledge about Georgia 'til we told him that we lived about half way between Kennesaw Battlefield and Chickamauga Battlefield. He knew his Civil War history.

Reel Foot Lake along the Tennessee-Kentucky border is popular with sportsmen throughout the year for hunting ducks. We saw duck blinds which are used in the winter. We were told this lake is rich in lore and legend and our navigator-guide was a good story teller.

As we continued on the River Road, we saw evidences of large farming operations. We also found more flood water interference – sometimes we got hard looks when we tried going where signs said "Local Traffic Only".

Amidst more Civil War relics, we spent the weekend with an exceptionally friendly group of regulars at Columbus-Belmont State Park. There was an anchor and a chain, we were told, had been used to stop wartime traffic on the river. We saw the Confederate Museum, a maze of fortifications and a beautiful overlook of the Mississippi River's present shipping lanes.

The major portion of Columbus, Kentucky was once situated along the river at bank level – subject to flooding year after year. After the major flood in 1927, the American Red Cross gave assistance in relocating the town on top of the bluff. We were told that most of the present buildings were moved.

King Mound at Bardwell, Kentucky is publicized as the "Buried City". It is a mound dwellers site which has been exploited by private ownership, but just recently has come under the auspices of the University of Kentucky. There seems to be plans for more scientific use of the site than has been true in the past.

We crossed the Ohio River into Illinois and made our way toward a park for a lunch stop, but water across the access road stopped us. However, we had a fun "lunch-stop-visit" anyway – even gathered up some of their "junk" to add to our "junk".

Sometimes we viewed the waters from afar and sometimes I almost wanted to tuck my feet under me to be sure they stayed dry. We crossed the Mississippi River into Cape Girardeau, Missouri. Just north of the city, we located the Trail of Tears State Park – yes, referring to the same "Trail of Tears" of Cherokee History. Our campsite was at the foot of a bluff with just the railroad between us and the river (closer look at the barges and their tows).

Back in "Cape" we went to the site of a Union Civil War Fort D. I understand there was a fort on each corner of the town, designated as A, B, C, D. Cape Girardeau has a very active Historical Association. One of their projects is The Glenn House. It was built in 1883 and has been restored to 1900. It has been maintained as a house museum since 1968. Mildred Vogelsang, the curator, spends much of her time in the office-library of the association located in a back wing of the house. We spent hours with her and enjoyed every minute of it. She let me poke around at all the quilts while Mulinix found the Victrola more interesting.

There is a Civil War Monument on the courthouse lawn – Union, not Confederate. From the courthouse door and looking down Themis Street, we could see the gate was closed – indicating that the river is still considered to be at flood stage.

As we left Trail of Tears State Park heading north, our reading indicated that we were nearing old German settlements. Roadside signs led us to The Oldtimers Agricultural Museum and Park at Altenburg. Here we met the Schmidts whose father came to the area from Germany in 1839. We met the father first, then the son, Ray, whose philosophy we admire:

"Behold the work of the old... let your heritage not be lost, but bequeath it as a memory, treasure and blessing... gather the lost and the hidden and preserve it for the children."

We hurriedly toured Ste. Genevieve, Missouri. It will celebrate its 250th anniversary in 1985. It was the first permanent white settlement west of the Mississippi and advertises itself as "Missouri's Most Historic Town" – providing examples of French Colonial vertical log houses as well as the brick step-gabled structures of the German immigrants - definitely a "tourist attraction". In the museum described as "containing varied collections of local memorabilia" we found a cradle with quilts piled inside. The lady at the desk knew nothing about the quilts.

A window display drew us inside "C & R Sales" – a store devoted almost entirely to crafts, with many beautiful quilts on display. Next door, a variety store called "U – Save Mart", seemed to deal extensively with quilts. They were everywhere and this store caters to the local Senior Citizens, thereby drawing on experienced quilters.

The Bolduc-Le Meilleur house was built about 1820. It was restored in 1967.

It was a couple of days later that a chance meeting with the keeper of Lyon Country Store, Carole Lohmeyer, lead to contact with Adele Zeugin, (Mrs. Harvey Zeugin), a local quilter and a retired shoe factory worker. Dell, as the locals call her, very graciously showed us one of her quilts with the edge of the quilt done in "Prairie Points". . . a technique not often seen in our area. Mrs. Dell says she usually counts on completing at least one quilt a month. I was impressed by the variety of things she produces and decided immediately that I wanted my name on her mailing list. She showed me the appliquéd butterflies – at that time still just in squares – but today my "Butterflies with Prairie Points" is one of my prized possessions!

Hermann is another tourist attraction. Deutschheim State Historic Site is dedicated to the German immigrant experience in Missouri, 1830's to 1870's. Presently Deutschheim (German Home) consists of two houses; The Pommer-Geutna House, where we found a day bed, quilts and in the garden, old-timey flowers blossomed. Just across the way was the second of the houses – Strehly House. Our Guide, Brian Horn, told us about some earlier activities here – the printing of a newspaper and the making of wine where a fine round caste was used. The kitchen garden contains ancient grape vines as well as a number of antique varieties of vegetables which are no longer available commercially.

Hermann's current wineries offer tours – mainly walking through cellars with lectures concerning their history and ending with a "tasting" amidst all the items they have for sale!

From Meramac State Park, where we had holed up for the Memorial Day weekend, we made a day trip to St. Louis, Missouri. We made a Flea Market stop, where we added 4 Readers Digest books to our collection and then we took the Anheuser-Busch Brewery Tour – more walking with the final destination – the gift shop.

After the brewery, Mulinix "homed in" on the Gateway Arch and the Riverfront. Street Construction and detour signs made our map almost useless! But by now we were getting pretty good at finding our way to the river and a long set of steps that went up to the base of the Arch. There were museums and shops and a "capsule transporter" to take you to the top where the observation room was 630 feet above ground. To the east was the historic waterfront and Illinois. To the west was downtown St. Louis. And then . . . there were the storm clouds that dumped one of the heaviest rainstorms we have ever been in. When we got back to Meramac, our campsite was completely under water. Mulinix donned sandals and a bathing suit to plug us in.

The next morning we introduced ourselves to a quilt at a neighboring campsite. I didn't think they were caring for their quilt properly. The two young couples from St. Louis promised to stabilize and nurture "Ye Old Quilt". That evening they brought us "Pudgy Pies" – filling between two pieces of bread cooked over the open fire.

Fischer Cave is one of Meramac's attractions. Mulinix took the tour; I stayed "home" and sewed. After Memorial Day weekend, we continued north and crossed the "wide Missouri" and on into Clarksville, Missouri. We found a sky ride to Lookout Point with a view of the river from the highest point between St. Paul and New Orleans. We got a bird's eye view of Lock and Dam Number 24; more tourist shops and one which contained a very rickety quilt frame. We saw jackets made from old quilts and always, views of the river. On one cold day, we spent enough time at the lock to see a tow "lock through". This guy seemed to be in radio contact with the pilot. The barges were, for the most part of the ones we saw, covered. The tug seemed no larger than those we'd viewed from the bluffs. Everything seemed to be routine business as the tug pushed his load through in two sections and then re-assembled it to move on down the river to the next lock.

Due to a breakdown on the road, the fuel pump had to be replaced. We met a young man, Bob, and his son, Josh, when they stopped to help us. Bob would take no pay, so I gave his small son some fruit and crackers. He took them and thanked me, but he would not eat them. He said he wanted to save them to eat with his daddy. I thought that was very sweet.

We went straight into Hannibal, Missouri, boyhood home of Samuel L. Clemens, better known as Mark Twain, and found a parts store Bob recommended. We replaced the fuel pump and added it to our inventory of spare parts.

We took a riverboat trip on the "Mark Twain", complete with dinner, good food, music, and a pretty waitress with a very short dress. Cruising on the riverboat made watching the river even more pleasant. James Hawkins, our captain for the "Dinner Cruise", told us that the Mark Twain would operate at Chattanooga, Tennessee during winter months and he assured us that even on the Tennessee River it will still be called the Mark Twain and will use its distinctive whistle.

We had live music with dinner and a waitress reminiscent of Riverboats gone by. After dinner we watched the setting sun from the upper deck. The next night we attended an outdoor drama, "The Reflections of Mark Twain". The River is actually part of the set. The action moves back and forth, upon and across. The players in the drama served as ushers and at the conclusion of the play, all the actors came into the stands to mingle with the audience.

Everywhere we found the landmarks of Twain's actual life and the settings of his writings used to catch the eye of tourists.. Amid an assortment of memorabilia in the Mark Twain Museum, was a familiar Bow Tie quilt.

We stayed in Hannibal for about a week. This was one of the main reasons for the trip. Plays, tours, museums, lectures, riverboat rides, and anything else we heard about along the way; we tried to see it all.

Down the street from the museum, at a shop called "Aunt Polly's", I looked at patchwork, but did not buy. Further down the street, at a shop selling antiques, I did make a purchase – Nine Reader's Digest books @ 10 cents each!

In an upstairs bedroom in the Mark Twain Home, there was a very distinctive "path" in the flower garden quilt. "Twainland Express" was a narrated drive through a number of Twain connected locations. The tour guide was passing out coats to brave souls who were in shirt sleeves. The one Mulinix received didn't exactly "fit" but he said it did help.

We saw the statue of Mark Twain on Cardiff Hill and then took another ride on the river – this time with a speed boat. Back at the dock, the Riverboat, Mark Twain, waited and we boarded for a one hour excursion complete with narration about the sights along the way.

Mark Twain was born at Florida, Missouri and a monument is about all that is there. Nearby, at the Mark Twain Birthplace State Historic Site, the two-room cabin in which Samuel Langhorne Clemens was born on November 30, 1835 has been preserved. Today it carries the mailing address of Stoutesville, Missouri.

June 2nd we backtracked, but actually "retracing" very few miles. We crossed the Mississippi into Illinois at Hannibal; turned south and re-crossed the great River into Louisiana, Missouri and spent most of the day at nearby Clarkesville.

The Apple House at Clarkesville, Missouri was where the Golden Raintree Festival was held on June 2nd and 3rd. They had a spot for wine tasting – with wine and bread offered at several different stations. You had to purchase a sticker which you put on your glass. Whenever you wanted to taste a certain wine, you lifted your glass, if they saw the sticker, your glass was filled. As usual, I reminded Mulinix to limit his intake. He had to get us back to the campground. We tried to collect two wine glasses from each winery visited. We collected enough for each one of our guest at our Christmas Eve dinner to have one.

I bought an Amish doll there as well as that deliciously fattening bread. Mulinix snapped a picture of me paying for it and the old gentleman let me know that he didn't like "pictures". But he didn't hesitate to accept my money complete with "pictures"! I also met a couple of ladies, Lucille Segress with a Double Wedding Ring in progress and Mary Williams setting out a variety of quilts for sale. There was a Folk Art display, mainly from the St. Louis Museum, presented by Melvin and Joann Barnes, local art teachers and members of Raintree Art Guild.

Nantucket Fisherman's Baskets – I asked the man how he happened to be so far from the North Atlantic. He said, "The church sent me here." His card read "Rev. Warren Gritzke" with an address in Liberty, Illinois – denomination not stated. All along our way as we routinely made weekend stopovers, we were able to locate Baptist churches. Occasionally they turned out not to be Southern Baptist, but most places we were graciously received and found the experiences very meaningful.

Clarence Cannon Dam impounds Mark Twain Lake. The U. S. Corps of Engineers camping facility there is a part of Ray Behrens Recreation Area. Our first night there we jokingly commented that our campsite came "with a private bath" – we were the only campers in our section. This was our base camp for all of the time in the Hannibal area. With our Golden Eagle camping pass, $4.00 a night, for full hook-up, made staying put attractive.

On June 4th, Day 26 of our Journey, we again began to follow the River Road northward. The other time was on the east side of the River. The tour of river-bottom farm lands was interrupted by "Road Closed" signs. More floodwaters – but before the days end, we had reached Nauvoo, (Beautiful City) the Mormon settlement. There are two groups in the settlement; one is the Reorganized Church of Jesus Christ of Latter Day Saints; the other is Church of Jesus Christ of Latter Day Saints. We had been cautioned by some people we met earlier, if we weren't careful we would only see the restoration efforts of only one group. We did manage to see both RLDS and LDS. We also saw well constructed wild life shelters for birds as well as musk rats and other things.

At The Homestead at the Joseph Smith Historic Center, we had a college student as our guide. The next morning, using a map secured in the RLDS section, we blundered into the LDS area of the restoration. At the restored Heber C. Kimball house, the first home in the area to be restored, we found beautiful quilting and were even given a pattern for the quilt they were working on. When the guide learned I teach quilting, she gave me several copies. Next we entered Lyon Drug and Variety. We were doing just fine, we thought – but the attendants there literally snorted when we pulled out our map. (It was a RLDS hand-out and this was LDS territory, remember.) When we were ready to leave, after getting a hand made block print of the store, they insisted on driving us to the Visitor Center.

During the tour of the Center, we saw a display of a woman's work with miniature Log Cabin Quilt and a mill rock outside the Blacksmith shop. Time spent beside the river turned up a fragment of broken glass for my growing collection of mementos and would you believe it carries the "Ball" trademark? Also, in our conversation with fellow tourists, we were introduced to Myrtle and Aaron Hansen, from Utah, teachers, possibly Mormons. He once sang with the Mormon Tabernacle Choir. He now teaches music. She teaches Art at the Indian Reservation.

At the Cultural Hall, antique quilts and a heritage quilt frame were on display. Our guide, along with his wife, presented a skit giving us insight into the Mormon story.

An interesting and unusual quilt called "Child's Crazy Quilt" was one we had never seen before. It had 40 items for a child to identify - a good learning tool.

On up the River, we found an impressive Indian Museum at Black Hawk State Park. In Moline, we toured the John Deere International Center; the building itself is Art.

At Lena, we made our first, though not the only, cheese factory visit. This is the company which has shipped us cheese orders, Kolb-Lena Cheese Co., Lena, Illinois. While camped at Lake Le-Aqua-na State Park, we toured Vinegar Hill Lead Mine, including the underground tunnels. Then at Badger Hill Mine and Museum, we found quilts in a display called "Jesse Cabin" with artifacts showing the life style in mining days. Our guide, Tommy Toley, seemed disappointed that we didn't want to don hard hats and "go underground" with him.

On Saturday, we went into Freeport, Illinois to deliver a quilting frame to Kathi Spaeth. Kathi already has two of our frames – both the large and the small. She had ordered another frame for her sister and we were delivering it to Kathi's house. We spent much of the day with Kathi. We had lunch at her house, visited and discussed local places of interest, then we went to Hartsville window shopping. The whole town was having a yard sale! We lucked up on the cooker like the one used to make the "pudgy pies" back at Meramac Park. I bought three – one for us; one for Gene; one for Victor. When we got back to Le-Aqua-na, we found our parking space had been taken – by a tree! The camp host was pulling a tree limb from the parking space. Incidentally we were told that the name for the park was the result of a contest. The explanation for the name is: Latin for water – Aqua; In the middle of Lena, thus Le-Aqua-na.

Stonefield is an 1890's Village and State Farm Museum at Cassville, Wisconsin. In the General Store there is a selection of quilts – one of which dates back to 1855. This was shared with us by Jean Adrian, a native of Cassville.

Usually the River Road was a small, very non-commercial looking route, but just after we crossed over the River into Minnesota, at Winona, we found the River Road to be a 4-lane highway right beside the River.

Mulinix kept his eyes watching for big trees. At Little Falls and Charles A. Lindberg State Park, we found several. We visited the boyhood home of the "flyer", Charles A Lindberg, Jr. while at the park.

We finally reached our Destination . . . but not before some frustrating contradictory route changes. This time, not for floodwaters but highway construction! A stop at a Cass County Museum in Walker saved the day. Not only did we find a marvelous nature museum, but an attendant who took the time to make total strangers understand the alternate routes available to us. I like their motto, also: "We are an arch between those who preceded us and those who will follow. Let us preserve and honor the best of yesterday, that it may guide us to a better tomorrow."

At first glance the landscape did not seem too exciting. But then we began to find "groves" of big trees, as well as sparkling clear lakes – of which our favorite was Lake Itasca, whose outlet is marked as the headwaters of the Mississippi.

On June 15th, Day 37 of our Journey, the notes said we had driven 3,125 miles since we left home. We stayed at Itasca State Park almost a week. It had a small stream – a big step would take you across it. There was nothing to do, but a few minutes of meditation on all the various views we saw of the Great River reminds us that small beginnings may result in great things.

As I remember, it rained sometime during each 24 hour period, but that didn't stop us. We went to all the special exhibits: a logging "sled" for use on "ice tracks"; replicas of early buildings which are a part of the account that here, prior to 1900, Minnesota's first Park was one of the nation's earliest State Parks to be set aside. We walked the woodland trails and climbed the fire tower for a "view from the top".

Itasca is a classical concoction derived from the Latin words for "truth" (veritas), and "head" (caput). There was much controversy before this spot was finally accepted as the great River's head. Tourists take turns photographing each other here. Our photographer was from South Carolina. There was a foot log for those not game enough to walk the rocks and convenient signs to let you show where you have been.

There was no marker noting the spot, but we took notice – the first time a public road "bridged the Mississippi"! Lake Itasca Post Office is near the North entry of the Park. We left the Park actually going farther North – following the course of the River. Our first "tour" stop was the Forest History Center SW of Grand Rapids. From the parking lot, you can see the river in the distance, the 1900 Logging Town, and a costumed guide.

We stopped at Mille Locs Lake and visited our 3rd Minnesota Historical Society Center: an Indian Museum. The major display depicts the four seasons. Our guide had served as a model in this display. From here I bought birch bark items and other Indian made products.

We crossed over into Wisconsin, but then doubled back, crossed the river again and spent one more night in Minnesota at O. L. Kipp State Park in Winona. We viewed the River from every lookout point and I bemoaned the fact that I didn't have the jacket I had just finished to photograph in this spot. I had to settle for a shot of the jacket made with the beaches at the back of Jonah's parking space.

We came down from that bluff and crossed the Mississippi going east, getting our last view of the Great River from Interstate 90. Incidentally, "great river" is what Mississippi means in the Algonquin Indian language.

Suggestions received at the Wisconsin Welcome Center helped us to avoid much of the major construction delays and helped us to find some off-the-beaten-path attractions – like a winery. Three days later, we were leaving from Brown County State Park in Indiana.

On day 47, we were in Indiana at the home of our former classmate, Jenny Puckett Howell. By this time we had used every one of the state maps that we collected for the trip; we had located most of the places of interest that we set out to see and had stumbled into many others that we knew nothing about when we started out. We had read and re-read our books and magazines featuring things along the way. We collected brochures and books to have to share, (and to keep) when we got back home.

In the afternoon, Jim's "50 cent Tour" as he called it, carried us to a local covered bridge, and to Melamora Canal reconstruction tourist town. It had shops of every kind, including quilt shops. We attended "early church" on Sunday so that they could take us to a popular smorgasbord (everybody knows we love to eat), and then to the Historical Facility, Mason Hall at Centerville, for the 12th annual Quilt Show.

Back at the Howell home, a few minutes at the family's fish pond furnished quite a catch of fish. Reluctantly, we left the Howell's, but we left loaded down with goodies: strawberries, vegetables, fish, and more. We drove less than 100 miles to our "folks" in Northern Kentucky. We took a day trip to the National Quilt Show in Oxford, Ohio, where Aunt Florence was a participant. It was one of the few "things we did" during the 10 days we spent with the Campbells. Jonah didn't move at all and many days, neither did we. The neighbors across the way, Luther and Lucy Marie Gray, brought in a family heirloom for us to enjoy. You see, not only do we find quilts as we travel, quilts find us, as well.

On July 6th, we drove through from Boone County, Kentucky to the Pocket Camping Area in Floyd County, Georgia, to attend the cemetery cleaning, a tradition since 1945. The next day, along with other members of the S.W. Puryear family, we cleaned the local cemeteries, spread a picnic lunch, visited with kith and kin, and by 3 P.M. were back at Route # 1, Kingston. Proud to be home and excited to find that while we were gone, Mulinix Road had been paved!

And so, on July 7, 1984, Day 59, Jonah's Journey '84 ended. The record shows that Jonah had traveled 5,011.6 miles. But through the kindness of friends and family, we had traveled even farther, with memories and mementos to treasure for days to come.

Chapter Fifteen

AS FAR NORTHEAST AS NIAGARA FALLS

Jonah's Journey # 3
May12-July19, 1987
4,968.0 Miles 13 Weeks

A send-off with an umbrella from Victor, Marty and Ben and a basket of snacks for the road from Ed and Doris Dickey, and we were on our way. We left home at 9:00 AM and got on the Blue Ridge Parkway going to its end. Around 4:00 PM, we arrived at Asheville, North Carolina Bear Creek Campground. Our only stops were at rest areas and Welcome Centers. Tennessee and North Carolina Centers had limited information on the Parkway. However, The Western North Carolina Farmer's Market across from the campground was very interesting.

The next day we visited the Biltmore Estate-House-Garden-Winery. It reminded me of an English estate I had seen on my visits to England. We had an interesting encounter with the lady at the desk in the entry of the house concerning plans for the cleaning of the tapestries—it would take five years! They are removed one by one and there are 125 rooms. We took the guided tours and after visiting the winery, Mulinix said, "I like mine better."

We left the Biltmore House and headed to Pisgah National Forest—the first Forestry School in America. We ran into heavy fog and checked into Forest Service Campground. The "Cradle of Forestry Gate" was closed due to the all-night rain. We almost missed what turned out to be a delightful, if drippy, half-day. Mrs. Donan Pierson took pity on us and took us under her wing. She saw to it, despite the rain, that we had a practically private tour of the facility. The movie was excellent and she helped us photograph the "King House" in the complex.

One of the stops we made was at the Stuart Nye Workshop. I learned that my original brooch is Stock # 1 on their listing! We visited Grove Park Inn, where we ate lunch in the parking lot; visited the Textile Museum, where Mulinix enjoyed antique cars while Lorraine Wilson had a ladder brought for me so I could see the "thread" on a Victorian quilt dated 1891 MEB. The thread appeared to be of velour or fringe, about ¼" wide and conched to make the flowers. The Folk Art Center had quilts ranging from $200 for a small wall hanging to $700 and up for regular quilts.

At Mt. Mitchell State Park we drove to the highest parking area. Fog was so thick. We walked to the lookout tower on the top and Mulinix climbed the tower. He said the view was "outstanding"—pure fog. Winter storms had damaged the trees and you could see evidence of tree cuttings to clear the roadway. The trees at the highest elevation are Frazier Firs. The fog kept us off the Parkway. We stayed down in the valley at a lovely campground, Clear Creek, until the fog lifted. We met the owners of the campground—an 80 year old couple who had operated the campground for 20 plus years—Mr. & Mrs. Carl D. Langston—very NICE.

When the fog lifted, we moved to the Northwest Trading Post where we saw "The Peaks of Otter" in Glendale Springs, North Carolina. We attended church, ate lunch in the grocery store parking lot, found a laundry-mat but could not hang clothes out because of the rain. We rode on into Virginia where we saw the Natural Bridge. They had a stupendous gift shop at the entrance. We received a proclamation of Honorary Citizenship of Lexington, Virginia. They were observing National Tourism Week. Along the walking tour, we saw the Stonewall Jackson House and Lee Chapel and Museum. We took a carriage ride by VMI, Stonewall Jackson Cemetery, and George C Marshall Museum.

At Montebello Camping and Fishing Resort, we went to Humpback Rocks Visitor Center. Fog kept getting worse and worse. We had intended to try to get to Big Meadow Campground, but stopped at Loft Mountain, after retracing our route. We missed it due to the thick fog and had to double back. We found no attendant so we signed ourselves in. When the fog lifted, temporarily, we became aware that our chosen site was beside the water tank! We began walking and found the Appalachian Trail entrance. We watched the fog shift and roll in.

Back on the Blue Ridge Parkway by 2:00 pm, we came to the 0.0 milepost. The Blue Ridge Parkway ended at Fishrock Gap, Virginia and the Skyline Drive began. Overnight, the fog lifted a little and by 6:45am we left Loft Mountain ahead of the fog. The only other thing we saw moving were the deer. We made a stop at Big Meadow Visitor Center where there were quilts on the walls showing leaves and plants that grow on Loft Mountain. We enjoyed the Hall of Valor at Battlefield Park, then checked into Rancho Campground. Endless Caverns were of interest to Mulinix, but I stayed in Jonah, sewing, shampooing, and making soup.

We went to New Market, Virginia and took their walking tour of "Bedrooms of American Museum and Pottery"—eleven different rooms of authentic furniture showing every period of American bedrooms from William and Mary (1680) through Art Deco (1930) housed in a restored historic 18th Century building.

Sunday we parked in the Methodist Church parking lot under the only shade tree around and went to the Baptist Church, Smith's Creek Regular Baptist Church. When we returned to Battlefield Park, we found Bushong House was open, finally. After visiting the Bushong House, we bought a "Cook" basket and visited Shenandoah Vineyard. The General Manager, Gerrard Mosner, explained "Finger Pruning" to us. We went to Haymarket, Virginia, visited Manassas Battlefield; walked the trails of the First Battle; bought a map for the riding tour of the Second Battle; then to the home of Frank and Suzy Parrot in Gambrell, Maryland where I picked up my checkbook. I had left home without it and Gene sent it to Frank's house. He kidded me about having almost all of his bills paid, but he needed more checks. We stayed there about a week. We visited Renwick Gallery but could not take pictures. We did secure quilts from the Indiana Amish Gift Shop. Frank and I walked 1 ¾ miles to the Community Garden. We gathered radishes and headed back home. After a late dessert of strawberries from their patch, I finished my quilt and called it a day.

Our itinerary for the new day started when we took Metro from New Carrollton to The Smithsonian and ate at The Court"—a restaurant exclusively for members of the Smithsonian. We took the tour-mobile route by the Lincoln and Vietnam Memorials, Washington Monument, The White House, U. S. Capitol and finally to Mount Vernon, the home of George Washington and lunch at "Rip's Country Inn".

On Sunday, we went to church at Emmanuel Baptist Church, in Gambrell, a very small, new church. We sat in folding chairs. Suzy went to Sunday School, which left Frank to take us. He had not been going to church. Suzy related to us later, that the next week Frank went with her and had been going every Sunday since. He continued going until his death.

Frank drove us around Fort Mead where he worked for RCA, a trip to Harper's Ferry, The Antietam Battlefield, and dinner at Hagerstown, Maryland. We left the Parrot's and slipped around Baltimore and stopped at the Pennsylvania Welcome Center to gather materials. Using one of the guides, we chose Prospect Valley Farm campground in Columbia—NOT SATISFACTORY! We located the "Old Mill Stream Camping Manor"—VERY NICE! While there, we took the time to service Jonah—waste out—water in. I did some laundry, washed my hair and called Ruth Martin. At Ruth Martin's suggestion we began the next day at the Mennonite Information Center. We secured a tour guide, Vivian Dinlinger, and drove 39 miles through farmlands—some Amish and some Mennonite. We bought a wall hanging at Hannah's Stoltzfoes Quilts and Handmades; at Minerva's there was a quilt in the frame; and at Eby Road—self serve BREAD!

Mrs. Vivian was an Eby. We photographed her old family house—no longer owned by the family. We saw water being pumped with a water wheel and wire. We noted telephones in small buildings outside homes and saw dairy cows up-stairs for milking in a three-story barn! We made two quilt stops, one roadside stand stop—self service, and one stop at the cheese factory to replenish our supply of cheese. About 40% of the Amish are farmers.

Before the trip ever started, Mulinix had told me, "Don't even ask to go to New York City." So I would not ask to go to New York City, but we went north of New York City to Boston. We stayed at a well-situated campsite where a bus came and went to Boston three times a day. We went on into Nova Scotia and then started back.

In Boston, Massachusetts, we had lunch at Hancock Shaker Village, west of Pittsfield. We did not feel the food measured up to Kentucky's Pleasant Hill. We located camping at October Mountain State Forest near Lea, Massachusetts. I washed my hair—no attendant—just put money in the box.

Staying on US 20, we saw men in the road indicating roadwork ahead. We learned what the "Breakdown Lane" was. It was the shoulder of the road which was reserved for problems. The signs read, "Do not drive in Breakdown Lane".

We arrived at Sturbridge where we fixed lunch and then began to tour. We felt lucky when we found a Quilting Party in progress in the Salem Towne House. We pieced a star with alternating plain blocks (of chintz)—quilting by the piece on stars, and "clam shell" on squares—marking with blue chalk and cardboard templates. We really enjoyed our time there. In the gift shop, I bought a purse—a Nantucket style basket.

Back on the road, we followed 20 into Littleton and the KOA Minuteman Campground where we stayed for four nights. From there we took the "Gray Line" tour bus into Greater Boston. We had to get up early for the tour bus.

Sheila Hancock, a member of "Bullock Hall Quilt Guild", and her family approached us at the end of our tour and referred us to a "Library" at Lancaster for a display of antique samplers. So, we went, but the Library was closed. We found an interesting General Store at Harvard with an extensive camera department. We bought film and then found a Barber Shop. We ate lunch at the Hotel near Common, then spent time watching Swan Boats.

In the afternoon we went to Salem and visited the House of Seven Gables, New England's only remaining 17th century mansion and the setting for Nathaniel Hawthorne's famous novel.

On Sunday, June 21st, we went to the First Baptist Church of Littleton. We did not attend. It started at 10:00 am and we got there at 10:50 am. We just rode the local roads and saw some interesting homes, then went back to camp to do some laundry, read the Sunday paper, and take a nap.

On Monday, we went to Lowell Massachusetts—we found the New England Quilt Museum closed. So we learned a little about the textile industry's early history. From the 1830's to WWI, the main product was cotton. Did you know there was such a thing as "brown cotton"? It was called "slave cotton" which could not be sold as quality cotton, but slaves could use it or sell it to each other. Today other industries such as a water power exhibit occupy the building. Another use for the old textile mills are apartments and tourism.

We visited National and State Parks with exhibits and tours. We rode the street car and the tour boat on the canals with a park-guided historical story of the mill and city. The tour information tied in with the film we had seen at Bucknell University. We camped on the ocean at York Harbour, in Maine, walked along the shore, even in the misting rain. It was our first view of the Atlantic.

We toured the Historic section of York, Maine—the Desert of Maine—an inland sand bar. We climbed Nubble Lighthouse Point for a better view. There was no outlet between the Desert of Maine and the Ocean. The west side of Mount Desert Island has less of the National Park, but many interesting spots.

The Mount Desert Oceanarium at Southwest Harbour, Maine was very good. We found more shells at Pretty Marsh than we had seen all week. We took pictures of Quilts at Bennett's Antiques in Trenton, Maine, then back to the KOA.

On June 24th, we stopped at L. L. Bean. It is open 24 hours. There were no sweaters that suited me. We tackled our first Maine Lobster at "Taste of Maine Harbour View"—gracious service, heavenly dessert—blueberry. By the end of the day, we camped at Camden Hills State Park. We walked the trail to the shore instead of the mountain. A couple from Pennsylvania joined us on our return trip and shared information on Acadia.

In Blue Hill, Maine, in our search of the "Cole House Quilts" place, we found and purchased a pillow made by a local artist. We also found a production pottery place. Rowantrees Pottery, with plates on hand. Rowantrees Pottery began as the outreach of a lady trying to teach others that they could do better for themselves than they were doing. The Pottery stood out. She taught them how to market it and at her death the Pottery was deeded to those in the Co-op. The restaurant there used the Pottery from the Co-op in their business.

Parking was sometimes a problem for Jonah. However, there was a local arts show at the Library, with parking available for Jonah. We had lunch at "Jonathan's" then back to Patton Pond KOA.

June 26th—we stopped at the National Park Information Center and bought a cassette tape tour of Acadia National Park. We drove all of the tour that was open to RVs and made all the stops. We walked on the shore and gathered shells and rocks. At the top of Cadillac Mountain, it was foggy and COLD. We bought a Sweet Grass basket at Abbe Museum that was made by the Passamaquoddy Indians.

Bedford Used Books was a service for anyone looking for a lost or out of print book. It was in an abandoned school with rooms, rooms, rooms, and books, books, books. They research and find lost books for anyone.

After attending Emmanuel Baptist Church in Ellsworth, Maine, we made a stop at the Bakery Shop then on to the Maine Agricultural Experimental Station (Blue-berry Hill). We got some materials but the office was unmanned. The Farm Tour was closed, as was the Fort O'Brien State Monument. We drove over the bridge into Canada for our lunch break and visited the Quoddy Head Lighthouse and crossed FDR Memorial Bridge to Campobello. Smartly dressed, gracious Canadian guides made our visit very nice. We only went to the park and ate. We did not exchange any money.

We went back to Maine for our last Meal of Maine Clam Chowder. We visited Farmington Antique Shop adjacent to the Rest Area where we "rested" and found a very worn Indian Basket—charge—fifty cents. We had seen Dexter Outlets all along the way and we finally stopped at one—didn't buy anything. We went on into New Hampshire when we realized our AC was not working. We had to go to East Montpelier, Vermont for AC service. We stopped at St. Johnsburg, Vermont and toured the Candy Factory on our way. We bought Maple Syrup and candy. When we arrived at Mekkilsen's, we found that there was no service possible for the AC, so we bought a new one. While there the son of the owner saw our purchase of 4 pints of maple syrup. He tried to reason why we had purchased four pints for $32, when we could have gotten a gallon there for $35. We told him we wanted the pints for gifts. It didn't seem to satisfy his reasoning.

We camped at Shelberne, New Hampshire yesterday. Today we camp at Shelberne, Vermont. The Camping areas were fabulous. The Shelberne Museum was described as a "collection of collections". We couldn't stay as long as we would have liked. The weather was getting worse and the fog caused us to seek a place to camp. Fog was so thick our vision ahead was very limited and getting more so all the time. We settled in at the Shawnee Springs Farm Campground for the July 4th weekend.

The campground owner, Jane Hyatt, told us of Amish in the area, so we went looking. We had a nice visit at Renneh. We found the "Mrs." making bread; one daughter quilting; another working with rug strips; the brother doing the weaving. Another daughter and husband, the Peacheys, operate a harness shop next door. All seem to live under the same roof.

There was a shop with fabrics, quilts, rugs, and we noticed some prints. We were told they don't use them, but they make them to sell. There was a white-on-white quilt with a center medallion of a quilted wreath and doves and twisted rope borders. We asked for some whole wheat bread. They only had half a loaf, but they let us have it. We waited for her to fill doughnuts—delicious! We ordered a loaf of white bread, fresh from the oven. As they put it in a bag they gave these instructions: "Turn it several times as it cools and don't close the bag until it is completely cooled".

The children ran to the barn when we first stopped, but were smiling at us before we left and stood at the window waving as long as we were in sight. These Amish were once in Pennsylvania. They had been there about seven or eight years. We understood there were eleven families in all. We saw several homesteads and their "wares" at the local gift shop.

In the week at Lancaster, we actually wore out the map! We visited "The Amish Farm and House" recommended to us by our "Tullie contact" in Atlanta, Betty Igou. She made our tour arrangements through her son who worked at the tour office. "The Amish Farm and House" was a typical Pennsylvania Dutch Farm in operation. We visited Anna Hurst's "Grandma's Quilts and Pillows" in New Holland, Pennsylvania, then "The Hershey Tour" which included "The Orphanage School" at Hershey—very impressive. The last stop on the tour was "The Winery".

Ruth Martin picked us up the next morning at 9:15 am and took us to "The People's Place" in Intercourse, Pennsylvania and on to a tour of shops: "The Old Country Store; "Antique Productions" where Ruth got embarrassed by a lady quilting in the store who would not let us take her picture. She also informed me that my friends and I should not make Amish Style Quilts lest we put her out of business—she was NOT Amish!

We left "Antique Productions" and went on to "The Village Pottery", "The Kitchen Kettle" and we bought a Mennonite wall hanging from Inger Henson then had lunch at "The Bird-In-Hand" café. We bought groceries at a large supermarket. We had had trouble finding one along the way. They were few and far between.

Typical pre-holiday situation—CROWDED!

On July 4th, Jonah did not move. I finished my skirt and Mulinix did a load of laundry. Someone was harvesting hay in an adjacent field and a lady was driving the tractor. Mulinix used the VCR. The farm owner, Robert Burt, came over. We told him we had enjoyed his Maple Syrup we had purchased from Jane. He offered to take us to the Sugar Shack and explain how it was made—VERY interesting. We also learned that Mr. Burt is on staff at Cornell University—his farm is very impressive. Agriculture is his expertise. The hay is going to a neighboring dairy farm.

July 5th, we went to Community Baptist Church in Poland, New York. Bulletin board listed 10:00 am Service—the bell rang—no service. We learned later, most of the area workers were "on vacation"! We rode by the dairy farm and made a stop at Burt's "Sugar Bush". I got a few leaves from Burt's "Sugar Bush". We were told the trees were native growth—not transplanted. We could see the rows where the sap had been collected. If the snow on the ground was deep, the rows were higher up on the tree. It takes from thirty to forty gallons of sap to make one gallon of syrup. We left Mr. Burt and did some laundry and made preparations for a "travel day".

Next day we met the Martins at "Henry's Classic Cars", went to "Central Market", then to the "Heritage Museum", and on to "Isaac's" for brunch. Soon after, we left the Martins and went to a huge Flea Market called "The Green Dragon". From there we went to Willow Street and the home of Mable and Jacob Harnish, another Tullie quilt contact we had met in Atlanta. Jacob took us first to "Country Auction" and we admired the quilts that were to be auctioned. The schools there receive no government funding. The quilt auctions provide the funding. They auction a quilt, someone buys it, and some time later, they may put it back in to be auctioned again. Some quilts may be auctioned several times. We watched for awhile. Jacob looked at his watch, as if on a time schedule, and said we needed to go. He said we would come back later. We went to the Craft days Program at Pennsylvania Farm Museum of Landis Valley. We ate lunch, went back to the Museum, and then back to the auction in time to see one quilt auctioned for $200. The top sale of the day, we were told, was a white-on-white with a school emblem in the center which sold for $1600. We left the auction and went back to the Harnish home where we put a quilt in Mable's frame.

On Sunday we attended services at Byerland Mennonite Church and then the fortieth Huber Reunion at "Shady Maple", the home of Chester and Arlene Eshleman. When we started to leave Mable's house, she put a bowl of food in my hand and said, "This is yours". Every woman was supposed to bring some food item. Rather than tell me, Mable had prepared a dish for me to take.

Food, fellowship, fun, and a concert of the Central Pennsylvania Gospel Band made a very enjoyable finale for our visit with the Harnish couple. We left Willow Street and the Harnish home and traveled to Paradise, Pennsylvania. We stopped in Basketville to shop for underwear and groceries. After a return trip to the Mennonite Information Center, we took a tour of the Hebrew Tabernacle reproduction. Afterward, we checked in at the "Old Mill Stream Camping Manor" for laundry and a shampoo.

Our next adventure was a suggestion from Mable's niece at the Huber Reunion. She told us how to get to Sunbury and the coal mining area. We took the mine and a nice museum tour at Ashland in our hard hats. We passed through Centralia, where the underground mine fire still burns. Many houses were boarded up. We found camping on the Island in Rapperock River.

In Lewisburg, Pennsylvania every museum in the area was featuring quilts and other handmade items. We located "Packwood House Museum"—a quilt exhibit gallery—where there were quilts throughout the house. The collections here were assembled by the former owner, a Mrs. Tetherston. Her paintings were also displayed. The Mifflinburg Historic Buggy Capital and Parkwood House Museum were two of the more interesting museums for Mulinix.

A short trip to the Overlook at Shikellamy State Park gave us a view of the rivers, the Island, the towns and the countryside.

We found workers at Fort Augusta Museum—it was not ready for visitors. We checked in at River Edge Camp.

Bucknell University in Lewisburg, Pennsylvania was offering some workshops that were of interest to Mulinix and me. We had registered for two or three each and they sent a list of materials we would need for the workshop we had been assigned. The only one that called for a needle and thread was one of Mulinix's. We kidded him about that for awhile.

Another of the workshops that Mulinix had registered for was Photography. When we actually got to Bucknell University for the workshop, nearly everyone in the workshop had a very expensive, but borrowed camera and they did not even know how to load the film. Mulinix spent most of his time teaching them "how to" with their cameras.

There were numerous quilt shows and fashion shows correlated with the many workshops being offered. The exhibits on campus opened at 11:00 am. We were allowed to take pictures and look to our hearts content. Seven-nine on our program had been listed as "Slides of the Project". Instead, we had a walk-through of the exhibit with the curator, and additional information about the "finds".

I fixed lunch in the school parking lot then we went to the Slifer House Museum. This Victorian House "living museum" is adjacent to Lewisburg United Methodist Homes. Once there was a hospital here, but it was relocated. Quilts here are from the Slifer House Collection with Victorians from the Oral Traditions Study added.

We found some baskets when we stopped in Lewisburg. We purchased some cheese, stopped at Sterner's General Store and bought some strawberries and a length of oil cloth for the table at the reunion. We saw the Corning Glass Center, where they hand-blow glass and the Rockwell Western Art Museum.

On day 56, we got to Niagara Falls in time to take the evening tour on the "Gray Line of Niagara Falls". We camped at the Plaza Court Motel AAA Campground. On the Canadian tour, we viewed the Falls with its rainbow! We rode through the surrounding area and saw a "whirlpool" and the cable car that crosses that spot. Just at nightfall, we saw the "Dancing Waters" show at Minolta Tower and went to the top of Skylon, a long cylindrical building, where we saw the lights of Niagara Falls, New York and Ontario.

July 7th, we spent the morning on the "American Tour" of the Power Plant, Whirlpool; Cave of the Winds Trip; rode on "Maid of the Mist" boat; and saw Goat Island. Our guide was Maurice. After lunch we rode a city bus to the "Turtles"—an Indian History and Culture Center. It was WONDERFUL! Also, we went to the "Rainbow Centre Shopping Mall"—only bought ice cream.

Day #58—We left Niagara Falls, New York and the Plaza Court Motel about 9:30 am. We drove across toll bridges, through Buffalo, and along Lake Erie. We made a brief stop in Evangola State Park at Lake Erie Beach, New York. Jonah began to act up. We drove through miles of grape vineyards—also orchards where you pick your own cherries and garden crops. We saw corn at roadside stands and being harvested. Just over the Pennsylvania line, we stopped for lunch and Mulinix worked on "Jonah". We found a parts place in the next town, North East, Pennsylvania. "IMPROVEMENT"—short lived.

We searched the Guidebook for campgrounds with a phone—Wednesday—call day for Victor. We decided on "Virginia's Beach Campground", North Springfield, Pennsylvania. On the spur toward the camp, we found the railroad crossing under major repair. We had to wait for about an hour. Our camp on the shore of Lake Erie provided an opportunity for us to walk along the beach! When the railroad crossing was fixed, we saw more grapes along the way to the grocery stop at Ashtabubar. We got onto Hwy. 534 at Geneva and saw more grapes and then much idle farmland. We saw some Amish farmsteads with pretty corn and cows.

We visited the Middlefield Cheese House and Ms. Miller at the Quilt Shop, "Stitch 'N' Post", gave us a map and directions to the Herschbergers. We learned a little bit about Swiss Cheese at the Middlefield Cheese House.

We found the Herschbergers—a family Rosie Wade had introduced us to when we visited her in Tennessee at the time we were delivering frames to Rosie. UPS delivered a big box of quilt tops from the Herschbergers while we were at Rosie's. Rosie was to look through them, mark what she wanted and send the rest back to them. Rosie picked one out, handed it to me and said, "This one is yours."

They were very gracious and we had a very nice visit. They showed us the frame they used and gave us "cool well water" to drink. We returned to the Cheese Factory and bought bread and more cheese. Along the way we spent the night at Spring Lake Park in Bristolville, Ohio.

On the road early, we had to make one roadside stop to "mechanic", but Rest Area stops were the only other stops made until we reached Walnut Lake Campground in Jeffersonville, Ohio. We did the laundry; shampooed my hair; and serviced the "Tank". There were preparations at camp being made for "Combine Demolition Derby" the next day. Weird!!

We went into Jeffersonville, Ohio for gas and paid the highest price of the whole trip—$1.189 per gallon. We planned to pick up Fish dinners at Aurora, Indiana's Kentucky Fried—found it was no longer there! We bought Fish dinners at "Flick's" in Lawrenceburg, on KY 20. When we got to Aunt Florence's, we found her hoeing tomatoes. We snuggled Jonah into his "slot" and felt we were home at last!

We kept the kids while Jo Ann and Bruce "ran an errand"—turned out they were picking up a NEW car! We had supper at the steak house with Billy and Mary included.

Day #62, Jonah did not move. We went to church at Bullitsburg Baptist Church. They had just celebrated their 193rd anniversary Ministry of Faith on June 7, 1987, but we heard all about it and then we heard the tapes made on that day. After church we had lunch at "Wildridge's" in Indiana—Billy included.

On July 13th, we had lunch at "Duff's"; watched some VCR of Niagara and Bill's "Band Performances". The next day, Mulinix made copies of the church celebration tapes while Florence cooked.

July 15th, we talked to Marty and heard the plans for the Puryear Reunion. We had lunch at "Captain D's".

July 16th, Billy and Mary carried us out for an evening meal at "Duff's". Afterward, we rode to see some of Bill's "Bulldozer Projects"—Joanne and the children, Tabby and Jonathan, came along. It was amazing how the children enjoyed "Duff's"!

Next morning we awoke to HEAVY FOG! Mulinix drove Florence to "Jenny's" to get her hair fixed. We left out for Georgia about 9:25 am. After stopping only at Rest Areas, we arrived at Cove Lake, Tennessee a little before 3:00 pm. We had supper at Park's

Restaurant—Florence insisted that we buy steaks. The Specialty of the House—fresh baked bread!

On the first Saturday after July 4 th it has been a tradition since 1975, to clean the Pocket Cemetery and Graveyard. From the first cleaning when they had to remove trees from the graves and a large patch of Johnson Grass, until today, when two of the sons of the occupants, now have a lawn service. They bring in their mowers and workers and by 10:00 am they are finished and ready for brunch. Victor supplies the food and drinks which come from our freezer and the 4th of July picnic leftovers—ham and biscuits, sausage and biscuits, chicken and biscuits, steak and biscuits, with the Puryear Brew or juices.

We left Cove Lake about 8:45 am. We were at the Georgia Welcome Center just after noon and arrived at the Pocket Cemetery about 2:15 pm. The "cleaners" had done a good job, as always.

We were pleasantly surprised to have Roland and Bessie Puryear join us for supper and for the Puryear Reunion the next day—also a tradition since 1975. The Puryear Reunion is always the third Sunday of July. We had 66 present at the Puryear Reunion at the Spring. There were 17 first cousins.

Day #69—HOME! We shared the last of our Amish bread and cheese with Victor and family and Gene and the boys. It's GOOD TO BE HOME!

Jonah's mileage: May 12-July 19, 1987—4,968.0 miles.

We had one more trip planned—going North on I-75 Interstate and following the route from the East Coast to the West Coast. However, one morning, Mulinix came in and said, "My face doesn't feel right."

"Uh-oh. What's wrong with your face?" I asked.

"Don't know," he replied. We never took anymore long trips.

Chapter Sixteen

FIFTIETH WEDDING ANNIVERSARY

1993 was a busy year, but the high point of the year was our 50th wedding anniversary with family and friends—some from far away—on December 23rd. Ray Thacker and his crew managed to provide food for the day.

I had made a small size quilt with mementoes of our 50 years together. We had an all-day quilting at 100 Mulinix Road. For those who were not interested in quilting, we provided a jigsaw puzzle with Victorian Crazy Quilt design.

Tullie Times

There were six or eight ladies who wanted us to continue our quilting activities. We met at 100 Mulinix Road once a month; that was once a month from January, 1985 to January, 1993 that we met regularly. Of course, there were times when we didn't get past the kitchen table. We swapped cooking recipes, for example as well as quilting and other needlework.

I could always count on this group when we were involved in quilt shows. I proudly called them "my Support Group". In fact, without them I could hardly tackle anything on time. We put on a Wine Tasting for a bus load of Atlanta History Museum's planned outings for its volunteers. Mulinix's wine was a true treat. Cheese crackers and the herb bread we called "tailings" was appreciated also.

Our scrapbooks show the participation at the Atlanta Council lasted from 1985 to 1993. During much of this same time, and longer, most of our group was also involved in the documentation of Georgia Quilts that, with a big help from Anita Weinraub resulted in publication of the book, Georgia Quilts.

Barnsley Gardens was trying everything to draw in customers. There were many special events: Re-enactments; Road Races; Handballs; Wreath Making; Easter Sunrise Service; Halloween Costume Ball; Photography Workshop; and Quilt Shows. I was involved in **"Quilts in the Garden—Barnsley Neighbors Show Their Quilts"**—the first of four quilt shows at Barnsley. It opened August 1st and 2nd, 1992. Each consecutive year there was a quilt show at Barnsley in August, and we kept the same theme throughout. I had very limited involvement in the fourth show in 1995. I had fallen and damaged my shoulder. I had to have some surgery done. A quite capable young lady looked at the previous year's book, picked up all the frames and things I used in setting up. They did a fine job.

I kept all the quilts made at Barnsley Gardens. I purposely bought all the materials, threads, needles, etc., so I could keep the quilts. One quilt top was given to me from one of my cousins, whose mother had made it for her. I quilted it and it was donated to the Atlanta History Society. It was the huge "Lone Star" pattern that covered the quilt top.

One of the more notable visitors to the Barnsley scene was the new owner of Barnsley Gardens, the Bavarian Prince, Hubertus Fugger.

Chapter Seventeen

FOOD AND FAMILY

In this household, food on the table was determined by which patches in our garden came in first. That depended on the weather day by day. If it rained and the ground was muddy, nothing could be gathered. Peas of some kind were served almost every meal.

One year it had not been pea picking weather for a couple of days. A tenant family on the farm used our same guidelines. So when there were no peas, the menu changed and we used previously preserved foods that were on hand—canned, frozen or dried.

One little girl, about seven, I guess, stood up and stretched to see the whole table and announced very loudly, "Where's the peas?"

Everybody laughed, but Bobbie didn't sit down until her daddy carefully explained why there were no peas on the table.

This family has the habit of putting a name on things. There's always an explanation—sometimes quite obvious. For instance, the spare bedroom is the "front" bedroom to me, but it is the "back" bedroom to Marty. Then there's the living room, which is the "dining room" or the "big room". The boys room was the "shed room". The "small room" is the smallest room in the house. Then there's the "sewing room" which is a catch all. The Generator is "George"; the red car is "Little Red"; the "Tractor Shed", the "Corn Crib", the "Cotton House" which is sealed so high up with a sealant so the cotton won't stick and you could measure a bale of cotton and go to the gin.

There are two cisterns. One cistern catches water from the barn and it is used to water the garden. The other is under the house and it was filtered with charcoal, then fine gravel, and finally a screen. I don't know if that one is still used or not.

One year a neighbor brought over a variety of new peas: blackeyes, speckled, purple hulled, and green peas. One person had frozen some and another person brought some in to cook simply marked Green's Peas. As a matter of fact, we had various freezings of peas that summer.

When the cook found the freezer and asked about all the peas, this was the answer. "Well, you remember that bushel that Leonard Green brought to us from his patch? They went into the freezer. We meant to put "Green's Peas" on them, but somehow it was shortened to fit the label on the carton. I guess, the "s" was left off. So now we have in the freezer—simply green peas which are crowder peas grown by Mr. Green."

We have always had fruits and vegetables from our own gardens. We have also enjoyed a variety of meats. In addition to that which is grown especially for eating, like pork, veal, chicken, even turkeys and other fowl, wild meats were also popular.

When the boys were old enough, they were given guns and taught how to shoot. Dogs were used to hunt birds and traps or boxes were used to catch rabbits.

There were certain rules—not necessarily written down, but never the less followed. For instance, nothing was killed just to be killing. It was for table use and they had to clean it and make it ready to give to the cook—at least field dressed. If you killed something, you ate it.

Raised animals were shared with neighbors, friends and family. Thus fresh meat was provided by others and when their killing time came, they shared with everyone. This plan worked when there was no refrigeration. Ham and shoulders were cured with salt. Sowbelly was buried in salt or smoked. One time they took some to Rome to be cured. They lost a lot of it. We never did that again.

I believe Mom and Dad were the only ones to cook the pig's feet. After cooking they would clean them and cook them again, then batter them and fry.

Mincemeat was made with the broth from pig's feet. You added huckleberries, apples, and fig preserves and you made mincemeat for pies.

Mother and Daddy they canned mincemeats and sausage; cooked it and put it in jars. They added grease and placed them upside down. The grease hardened and sealed the lid.

Most of the Mulinix men take great pride in cooking. Vic's specialty is Bar-B-Q. When he and Marty lived in the Atlanta area,

Vic built backyard BBQ Pits and invited the neighbors to come. It's an activity that continued when they moved here. First it was for just a few neighbors, co-workers and family. Over ten years ago, he had one for his dad's 80th birthday. It was done at his current shop. That group was mainly family members and notices were sent out for the 4th of July. We held to that date.

One year the 4th was on Sunday. We invited all of both Kingston Baptist Church and Kingston Methodist Church. It has been, what I call, "YA'LL COME!"

The crowds grew—some have come to every one. But there will be some who will be here for the first time. Word spreads—from doctor's office to the grocery store.

Vic has one man who comes to help cook, but leaves on the 4th. His wife's birthday is on the 4th and they celebrate that each year. However, for two days, he and others are here turning the meat every hour, night and day.

One year, we forgot to put the bread on the table. We found it later burned to a crisp. Then, one year I bought two bags of salad greens and dressings, just in case we needed extra. We found those in the refrigerator two or three days later—unopened.

For 2012, friends and family from far and wide came. Some of my quilting friends felt that my 90th birthday warranted a celebration. I believe it was Anita Weinraub's idea to make a quilt of messages. As I understand it, there were over 300 4 x 4 inch squares of cloth sent with the invitations. If they wanted to, they could write something and return it to Anita to be included in the quilt top. I believe there were around 130 returned. In the center of the quilt top is a picture of me Victor found in his dad's wallet. It had gone around the world with Mulinix during the time he was in the service.

Of course, I had no clue. I had made the family promise not to make a big to do for my birthday which they had done for Mulinix's. (They had made a quilt and had everyone sign it.)

When I asked Victor to read the invitation to me, he read only the part about the picnic. He omitted the information about the birthday.

A group of women came later and quilted to finish it. It hangs in my living room. I guess, I expected a little something for my birthday, but never the scope of this quilt.

Believe me, it is a truth that nature takes away our playthings one by one. With me the first thing was my vision with macular degeneration. When first discovered, I was told that it would not get any worse. But it did. A year later this medical professional admitted that it was still worse.

I was fortunate to have a friend who began to help the family with the cooking and cleaning. Because of her interest in reading, she managed to find at least 45 minutes to an hour each day to read to me. Our house is stuffed with books, magazines, and stuff I intended to read "one day".

Places and people came alive in the stories of Eugenia Price—local places like the Etowah River and other historical places that Ms. Price used in her books. We shared memories of these and enjoyed discussing them when she was making appearances in our area.

Most recently, nature seems to be taking my hearing. A short while ago a friend was planning a birthday surprise for a mutual friend. She whispered in my left ear and I couldn't hear a word. It is true that we aren't always aware of how nature works. We must try to take things one day at a time and enjoy family and friends and be faithful to the work the Lord has provided for us.

Chapter Eighteen

THE FIGHT IS ON

With as many brushes with death as I have had, who would have predicted Mulinix would go first? We went for our Regular check-ups. Dr. Brad Ward was checking my "vitals" while the nurses were checking Mulinix's "vitals". A frustrated nurse opened the door and said, "Doctor, we can't get a pulse."

Dr. Ward turned and went immediately to Mulinix with me on his heels. He worked with him for an eternity, it seemed to me, but it was actually only a few minutes. He finally got a pulse, but he said, "We need to get him to a heart specialist." He made a call but was unable to get Mulinix seen that day. However, he did manage to set up an appointment for the following morning.

When we saw the cardiologist, he asked when we had been referred to him. We told him we had seen our Doctor the day before but his office had not been successful in getting a appointment with you until today. He responded, "But this is an emergency. Had I seen him yesterday, I would have operated yesterday. Since I am seeing him today, I will operate today," and sent us directly across the street to the hospital.

On August 12, 2009, Mulinix had his pacemaker surgery. In conjunction with that, when x-rays of his chest were made a mass was seen in his right lung. A biopsy was performed on the right and left chest areas. We had been told they were pretty sure it was malignant. The biopsy confirmed their thoughts. We talked to all the doctors who were involved with Mulinix's possible treatments. Each doctor had his say.

Gene said, "We have to consider the quality of life, too."

I asked the doctors, "If you do the "treatments", how long?"

They all agreed, "About a year"

"If you don't do the treatments, how long?" I asked.

Again, they all agreed, "About a year, maybe less."

Mulinix sat shaking his head the whole time. Finally, he spoke, "I don't want any of it. Just leave it alone." So after all the consultations with the medical specialists and the family had their input, it was Mulinix who made the final decision that there would be no aggressive treatment done.

Dr. Brad contacted Hospice to check up on Mulinix and to keep him abreast of his condition through regular reports from Hospice. (I called Dr. Brad our "quarterback". He called the shots—we did as we were advised.) He made appointments with specialists and Hospice as needed.

The doctors thought Mulinix would need oxygen, so they ordered it for him. When it arrived, Mulinix said, "They're pushing me. I don't need it." We had them take it away.

One of the Hospice girls, Amanda, who had been caring for Mulinix, had been sick and gotten behind on some of her workload. I asked her to eat with us. She declined, saying she would gulp down a sandwich as she worked. I looked at her and said, "No! You will eat with us."

We sat down to eat. Mulinix had gotten to where he would store three bites in his cheeks. However, when he swallowed, he upchucked. I apologized to Amanda for the rude way I had spoken to her, but I wanted her to see what was happening. She told me not to apologize, that she needed to know this.

About one day before his death, he began using oxygen. We went to church on Wednesday.—Mulinix got sick at church. Thursday is just a blur for me. He died at home on Friday, December 30, 2011. He had lived two and one-half years after his diagnosis and had not been sick or had not complained of being in pain until the last two or three weeks. He did finally admit to being tired. The last thing he said that I understood was, "Thank you, Thank you, Thank you." About a minute later, again, "Thank you, Thank you, Thank you."

Victor realized before I did that Mulinix had died. He called Pastor Jimmy, and he and Vanessa came and stayed until late. Victor called hospice and their nurse called the Funeral Director. Marty got Mulinix's clothes, which had been laid aside years ago and they confirmed the arrangements which had been made earlier.

We had his funeral the day after New Year, January 2, 2012 at Kingston Baptist Church—11:00 AM. Pastor Jimmy Garland officiated. Mulinix was buried with full Military Honors in the Kingston Cemetery. R. Dudley Barton and Son were in charge of the arrangements.

Sylvia Malone, who played the organ at the service said I had asked her to play from the old hymnal "When They Ring Those Golden Bells" back before she married. I don't remember that, but I do appreciate the job she and Phyllis Casey did with the music.

I guess we knew when the malignancy was confirmed, it was possibly the gradual beginning of the end. However, we did not live in dread, but enjoyed the time and the quality of our time together.

Victor retired at age 62, in 2009, to help care for his Dad. Currently, his main activity is "looking after me" since his Dad's death. Although Marty lives in Lithia Springs during her work week, since 2009 their address is considered as 100 Mulinix Road. They are active in some history, art and photograph associations in Cartersville as well as holding several responsible positions in Kingston Baptist Church.

There is no way I can ever feel that I have told all about my life. I am sure I have left out many things. If you think of something that warrants an addendum, please let me know.

All in all, I have had a good life with advantages and opportunities that far exceeded that which my financial station afforded. I agree with S. W.—that somehow there is a correlation between a good life and a good education.

S. W. is gone, but as I've thought about it and looked back over the years, I realize that his descendants are actually carrying on his philosophy. Many are, or have been, involved in education. Others have attained the education necessary to go into different areas and have made better lives for themselves, their families, and mankind.

Large complexes are equipped with labs and classrooms with TVs and computers. Classes are offered which can prepare students for some kind of job even if they are financially unable to go to college.

Better transportation for everyone, including students—either in the big yellow school buses, or parents taking them, or even their own personal car. The roads now are paved roads in most areas.

S. W. took a unique way to provide what he felt was a better life—Education. His respect for education can be seen in many of his descendants who attained more schooling than he did.

Notice the students you see preparing for a better life—teachers who are well prepared and who offer students every help.

Our economy is tied to our educational opportunities. My life, its quality and my enjoyment of it, in my opinion, prove S. W.'s philosophy of a better life through education.

Education is only one of the building blocks to a better life, but I believe it is the cornerstone of the foundation—where we must start.

As for me, my productive years are gone. It's too late to lay up treasures where dust and moth cannot destroy. I must stay the course and wait patiently to meet the Lord, and wait impatiently to greet Mulinix.

CPSIA information can be obtained at www.ICGtesting.com
Printed in the USA
LVOW12*0941101213

364673LV00001B/3/P

9 781491 839232